The Hospitality Playbook

Leadership Coaching

By Von Nelson

About This Book

The hospitality industry is bleeding talent. This book stops the bleeding.

With a turnover rate of 73.8%, more than double any other major industry, hospitality has normalized a revolving door that costs billions in lost productivity, decimated service quality, and exhausted the managers left behind to pick up the pieces. We've accepted this as "just how it is." It's not.

The Hospitality Playbook offers a different path. Not through gimmicks, pizza parties, or empty promises about "family culture," but through a proven coaching framework that transforms how we lead, develop, and retain the people who make hospitality work.

This book bridges 35 years of frontline hospitality experience with cutting edge research in organizational psychology and leadership development. It's built on a simple truth: people don't leave jobs. They leave managers who don't develop them, cultures that don't value them, and organizations that offer no path forward.

What You'll Find Inside

Five strategic "plays" that address the root causes of turnover:

- **The Culture Play** shows you how to diagnose and intentionally shape workplace culture that retains talent, not repels it.
- **The Leadership Play** transforms managers from taskmasters into coaches who develop people, not just manage schedules.
- **The Feedback Play** replaces annual reviews with real time developmental conversations that improve performance without triggering defensiveness.

- **The Career Path Play** creates transparent growth trajectories that combat hospitality's reputation as a dead-end industry.
- **The Inclusion Play** builds psychologically safe environments where every team member, regardless of background, feels genuinely valued and heard.

Each play is backed by research, illustrated with real world examples, and designed for immediate implementation. No theory without practice. No platitudes without proof.

Who This Book Is For

This playbook is written for the people in the trenches:

- General managers tired of training replacements instead of building teams
- HR directors searching for retention strategies that work
- Restaurant owners watching their best people walk out the door
- Hospitality leaders who know there must be a better way
- Anyone who believes that hospitality can be both a career and a calling

Why Now

The hospitality industry stands at a crossroads. Labor shortages aren't temporary. Worker expectations have fundamentally shifted. The old playbook of "deal with it or leave" doesn't work anymore. We need a new approach grounded in how people stay, grow, and thrive.

This book is that approach. Evidence based. Battle tested. Ready to implement. **The game has changed. Your playbook should too.**

Dedication

To My Family

This book is dedicated to my family, the steady foundation that reminded me who I was when life took an unexpected turn. Family is not defined by whoever stays, but by those who stand beside you when the storms come and the silence settles. When someone walks away, it can break you or build you. I chose to rebuild. What was meant to weaken me instead revealed my strength. Through that pain, I found clarity, resilience, and a deeper understanding of what truly matters.

To my family who stood firm, who believed when belief was hard, and who helped me rise, I owe you, my gratitude. This book is proof that endings can become beginnings and that sometimes the greatest growth comes when the path you planned falls apart.

To Coach Scott

Some mentors teach. Others transform. Coach Scott, you redefined what mentorship means. Your influence reached far beyond the field, reshaping not just how I coach, but how I live. You showed me that potential lives not only in victory, but in the discipline, effort, and spirit required to continue when victory seems impossible. True coaching, you demonstrated, nurtures character and integrity alongside skill. Growth isn't a destination; it's forged through continuous learning, inevitable setbacks, and relentless determination. Your passion for excellence, your commitment to development, and your belief in me have become woven into the DNA of *The Coachable*. This book carries forward your legacy. In honoring you, I honor every lesson that made me not just a better coach, but a better person.

To the World of Hospitality

Hospitality is an intricate dance of resilience, service, and dedication: a world where each day brings fresh challenges and rewards, where every person plays a vital role in creating experiences that last a lifetime. To the industry that gave me both professional purpose and personal fulfillment: thank you. In every shift worked, every service provided, every team I've led or joined, I've witnessed how hospitality shapes lives, builds communities, and creates moments people carry with them forever. This book honors those who work tirelessly, often behind the scenes, giving their best so others feel at home. *The Hospitality Playbook* is my tribute to this industry and the extraordinary individuals within it, each of whom taught me that true success lives in the details, in consistency, and in the shared passion for making a difference.

Outline

Chapter 1: Introduction

Chapter 2: The problem with Hospitality

Chapter 3: The Coachable

Chapter 4: The Playbook.

- The Culture Play
- The Leadership Play
- The Feedback Play
- The Career Path Play
- The Inclusion Play

Chapter 5: Applying Coaching techniques to the Hospitality Industry

References

Professional Biography

Chapter 1: Introduction

The Why

The Cost of the Revolving Door

In 2023, the hospitality industry faced a crisis that most leaders had normalized: an average turnover rate of 73.8% (U.S. Bureau of Labor Statistics, 2023) more than double the cross-industry average of 32% (Work Institute, 2023). This isn't merely a staffing inconvenience; it represents a fundamental breakdown in how we lead, develop, and retain talent. Every departure carries hidden costs: decreased service quality, eroded team morale, lost institutional knowledge, and financial burdens ranging from $5,864 for hourly positions to over $50,000 for management roles when accounting for recruitment, training, and productivity losses (Boushey & Glynn, 2012; People Management Association, 2022).

Yet despite decades of acknowledging this problem, the industry continues to treat turnover as inevitable rather than solvable. *The Hospitality Playbook* challenges this assumption. Drawing from organizational psychology, leadership theory, and 35 years of frontline experience, this book presents a coaching framework for building resilient, high performing hospitality teams.

Why Coaching? The Theoretical Foundation

The choice to frame leadership through a coaching lens is deliberate and research backed. Transformational leadership theory, pioneered by Burns (1978) and expanded by Bass (1985), demonstrates that leaders who inspire, develop, and individually consider their team members to generate higher performance, job satisfaction, and organizational commitment. More specifically, coaching leadership defined by Hamlin, Ellinger, and Beattie (2006) as "a developmental process through which individuals are helped to achieve their personal and organizational goals" has shown significant positive correlations with employee retention in service industries (Liu & Batt, 2010; Ellinger, Ellinger, & Keller, 2003).

The hospitality industry's unique challenges (high stress environments, irregular schedules, emotional labor demands, and often limited career visibility) make coaching leadership particularly relevant. Research by Jung and Yoon (2015) found that hospitality employees under coaching oriented leaders reported 41% lower turnover intentions and significantly higher organizational commitment compared to those under traditional management approaches.

The Retention Crisis: Beyond the Statistics

While the 73.8% turnover figure captures attention, it obscures important nuances. Turnover isn't distributed equally: front line positions experience rates exceeding 80%, while management roles average 35 to 40% (American Hotel & Lodging Association, 2023). This creates a vicious cycle where inexperienced managers lack the skills to develop and retain their teams, perpetuating instability.

The causes are well documented. Herzberg's Two Factor Theory (1959) distinguishes between hygiene factors (wages, working conditions) and motivators (recognition, growth, meaningful work). While the industry has slowly addressed compensation gaps post pandemic, research by Davidson, Timo, and Wang (2010) reveals that hospitality workers cite lack of career development, poor management relationships, and feeling undervalued as primary departure reasons: all motivator factors that coaching leadership directly addresses. Furthermore, Lee and Way's (2010) study of 308 hotels found that high involvement work practices including extensive training, empowerment, and developmental feedback reduced turnover by 19% while simultaneously increasing guest satisfaction scores. The evidence is clear: retention isn't about perks; it's about creating environments where people feel developed, valued, and connected to purpose.

The Playbook Framework: Five Strategic Interventions

This book structures its approach around five evidence based "plays," strategic interventions targeting the root causes of turnover and disengagement:

The Culture Play examines organizational culture as a retention tool. Drawing from Schein's (1985) model of organizational culture and Cameron and Quinn's (2011) Competing Values Framework, this play provides tools for diagnosing and intentionally shaping workplace culture. Research by Sheridan (1992) tracking 904 employees across six years found that culture fits predicted retention more powerfully than job satisfaction or organizational commitment.

The Leadership Play develops coaching competencies in managers. Based on the GROW model (Whitmore, 2009) and integrating emotional intelligence frameworks (Goleman, 1995), this section transforms managers from taskmasters into developers of talent. Studies by Wong and Laschinger (2013) demonstrate that authentic leadership behaviors reduce burnout and turnover intentions by up to 30% in healthcare and hospitality settings.

The Feedback Play establishes continuous communication systems. Traditional annual reviews have failed hospitality workers who need real time coaching in dynamic environments. This play implements Kluger and DeNisi's (1996) Feedback Intervention Theory, showing how to deliver developmental feedback that improves performance without triggering defensive reactions, critical in an industry where 67% of employees report receiving inadequate or poorly delivered feedback (Hospitality Employee Survey, 2022).

The Career Path Play creates transparent growth trajectories. Applying Schein's (1978) career anchor theory and Super's (1980) life span development model, this section helps organizations build visible career ladders that combat the industry's reputation as a "dead end" job. Research by Choi and Joung (2017) found that perceived career growth opportunities reduced turnover intentions by 52% among hotel employees.

The Inclusion Play builds psychologically safe, diverse teams. Integrating Edmondson's (1999) psychological safety framework with Nembhard and Edmondson's (2006) research on status differentials in hierarchical industries, this play addresses how marginalized employees (particularly in an industry where 75% of workers are women or people of color, Bureau of Labor Statistics, 2023) can feel genuinely valued and heard.

Finally, Addressing the Why

My Research Practice Bridge

My dissertation research examines how specific leadership behaviors influence turnover intentions among hospitality workers, seeking to identify the precise mechanisms through which coaching leadership reduces departures. This book serves as a bridge between that academic inquiry and practical application, translating theory into actionable strategies that general managers, HR directors, and team leaders can implement Monday morning. The hospitality industry stands at an inflection point. Labor shortages, changing worker expectations, and increasing operational complexity demand a new leadership model. This playbook offers that model not through platitudes about "treating employees like family," but through evidence-based practices that transform managers into coaches and organizations into places where talented people choose to stay, grow, and build careers. The following chapters break down each play in detail, providing diagnostic tools, implementation frameworks, case studies, and reflection exercises. Whether you manage a 50-room boutique hotel, oversee operations for a restaurant chain, or a small hospitality business of any kind, these strategies will help you build the resilient, high-performing teams that exceptional service requires.

The game has changed. It's time our playbook did too.

Chapter 2: The Problem with Hospitality

From a Coach's Viewpoint

The hospitality industry faces a multifaceted crisis rooted in structural failures of leadership development, unsustainable work demands, and the rapid integration of technologies that managers are ill-prepared to navigate. With a 73.8% annual turnover rate (U.S. Bureau of Labor Statistics, 2023) and burnout rates reaching 80.3% among hospitality workers (Paychex, 2023), these challenges are no longer isolated incidents but systemic dysfunctions requiring strategic intervention.

This chapter examines three critical dimensions of the hospitality crisis: imposter syndrome among managers promoted without adequate leadership preparation, the burnout epidemic fueled by work-life imbalance, and the disruptive impact of artificial intelligence on management practices. Each represents a distinct yet interconnected failure in how the industry develops, supports, and retains its workforce.

Imposter Syndrome: The Leadership Competency Gap

In 2025, a groundbreaking study by Bournemouth University and The Burnt Chef Project revealed that 75% of professional chefs worldwide reported suffering from imposter syndrome, with many attributing their success to luck rather than competence (Giousmpasoglou, Marinakou, Papavasileiou, & Hall, 2025). This finding illuminates a broader pattern affecting hospitality managers across all segments. First identified by psychologists Clance and Imes (1978), imposter syndrome describes a psychological pattern where individuals doubt their abilities despite evident success and harbor persistent fears of being exposed as frauds.

The hospitality industry's promotion practices create ideal conditions for imposter syndrome. Research confirms that organizations routinely elevate employees based on technical proficiency while neglecting the soft skills essential for effective leadership: emotional intelligence, communication, conflict resolution, and team development (Forson, Hao, & Cheung, 2025). A manager who excels at inventory control or service speed may flounder when asked to coach struggling employees, navigate interpersonal conflicts, or inspire team cohesion.

The Manifestations and Costs

Imposter syndrome manifests through predictable behavioral patterns. Managers experiencing these feelings often resort to micromanagement to maintain control, avoid giving constructive feedback to prevent vulnerability, or emotionally disconnect from teams to protect themselves from perceived inadequacy (Bernard et al., 2002; Chrisman et al., 1995). Research using the Clance Imposter Phenomenon Scale demonstrates that managers with high imposter scores exhibit significantly elevated anxiety, depression, and emotional instability compared to confident peers (Vergauwe et al., 2015).

The organizational costs extend beyond individual managers. Here's what happens: managers struggling with imposter syndrome don't ask for help. They hide. They cover their insecurities by projecting false confidence, micromanaging to maintain control, or isolating themselves from their teams (Thompson et al., 1998). They push away mentorship, refuse coaching, and decline development opportunities because admitting they need help feels like confirming their worst fear: that they're frauds who don't belong in leadership.

This defensive posture creates a toxic cycle. Teams sensing their manager's insecurity lose trust and engagement, even if they can't articulate why something feels "off" (Vergauwe et al., 2015). When leaders aren't vulnerable, won't admit mistakes, and won't accept support, psychological safety evaporates. Service quality suffers because the team is managing their manager's fragility instead of serving guests (Nembhard & Edmondson, 2006).

The research confirms what we see on the ground: imposter syndrome correlates with increased turnover intentions, with affected managers more likely to experience burnout and leave their positions prematurely (Forson et al., 2025). They quit before they can be "found out." A 2024 study found that 71% of CEOs and 65% of senior executives across industries experience imposter syndrome, with 52% of first level supervisors reporting similar struggles (Korn Ferry, 2024). These aren't isolated cases. This is the silent epidemic of hospitality leadership.

The particularly insidious aspect? The better someone is at their job, the more likely they are to experience imposter syndrome (Clance & Imes, 1978). High achievers attribute success to luck rather than competence, so each promotion intensifies their fear of exposure. They work harder, sleep less, and isolate themselves more, all while believing that if people truly knew them, they'd see through the facade. This perfectionism and fear of being exposed directly contributes to burnout and turnover in leadership positions (Vergauwe et al., 2015).

The Structural Root: Promotion Without Preparation

The problem originates in flawed talent development systems. When organizations promote based solely on technical ability, they implicitly communicate that interpersonal skills matter less than operational efficiency. This message contradicts the reality that hospitality leadership fundamentally involves developing people, not just managing processes. Yet many organizations provide minimal leadership training post promotion, expecting managers to "learn on the job" through trial and error (McLean et al., 2005).

This sink-or-swim approach creates a self-perpetuating cycle. Managers lacking confidence in their leadership abilities struggle to develop their teams, leading to disengagement and turnover. New hires enter the same system and, upon promotion, replicate the pattern. The entire organizational culture becomes infected with insecurity, where open communication and innovation are suppressed (Clance & Imes, 1978; Vergauwe et al., 2015).

The perfectionist trap exacerbates the problem. Many managers, especially those new to leadership, believe they must possess all answers and perform flawlessly. In hospitality, where guest satisfaction scores and online reviews provide constant performance feedback, this pressure intensifies (Giousmpasoglou et al., 2025). Managers interpret minor service failures as personal inadequacies rather than learning opportunities, deepening their imposter feelings.

Beyond Individual Psychology: Organizational Solutions

Addressing imposter syndrome requires systemic intervention, not individual therapy. Organizations must fundamentally rethink how they identify, develop, and support leadership talent. First, hiring and promotion criteria must explicitly value soft skills alongside technical competencies. Emotional intelligence assessments, behavioral interviews focusing on past leadership challenges, and 360-degree feedback should inform promotion decisions (Goleman, 1995).

Second, structured leadership development programs must replace ad hoc learning. Research demonstrates that coaching oriented leadership development significantly reduces imposter feelings while improving manager effectiveness (Ellinger et al., 2003; Hamlin, Ellinger, & Beattie, 2006). These programs should include:

- Formalized mentorship connecting new managers with experienced leaders
- Skills training in emotional intelligence, coaching conversations, and conflict resolution
- Peer learning cohorts where managers discuss challenges in psychologically safe environments
- Regular feedback loops normalizing struggle as part of growth

Third, organizations must cultivate growth mindset cultures where mistakes are reframed as learning opportunities (Dweck, 2006). Leaders at all levels should model vulnerability by sharing their own developmental journeys, explicitly acknowledging that leadership competence is built through practice, not innate talent.

Work-Life Imbalance: The Burnout Epidemic

Hospitality's burnout crisis stems from fundamental industry characteristics that create unsustainable work conditions. Unlike industries with predictable schedules, hospitality operates continuously, demanding evening, weekend, and holiday coverage. Employees regularly work irregular hours with minimal advance notice, making personal life planning nearly impossible (O'Neill & Xiao, 2010).

The 2025 OysterLink Worker Burnout Report documented the crisis through comprehensive industry data. Key findings reveal:

- **Long working hours:** 70% of hospitality workers report regularly working over 40 hours weekly, with 30% exceeding 50 hours
- **Insufficient breaks:** 65% cannot take adequate breaks during shifts due to understaffing and high customer demand
- **High stress environment:** 80% describe their work as "highly stressful," citing demanding customers, fast pace, and pressure to maintain service standards
- **Physical demands:** 75% report physical exhaustion from prolonged standing, lifting, and repetitive tasks
- **Inadequate compensation:** 60% feel their wages don't reflect their workload, especially when tips fluctuate or are inadequate
- **Manager unsupportiveness:** 67% report that requests for shift adjustments are

dismissed, fueling frustration (OysterLink, 2025)

The Cascading Consequences

Burnout manifests as emotional exhaustion, the depletion of emotional resources through continuous work demands (Maslach, Schaufeli, & Leiter, 2001). Research in hotel settings demonstrates that emotional exhaustion significantly predicts decreased job satisfaction, lower organizational commitment, reduced customer orientation, and increased turnover intentions (Karatepe & Aleshinloye, 2009; Lee et al., 2012).

A comprehensive study of UAE hotel employees found that burnout predicts intention to quit both directly and through psychological distress, which partially mediates this relationship (Al-Abri et al., 2023). The financial implications are substantial: when accounting for lost productivity, recruitment, and training costs, burnout driven turnover becomes one of hospitality's largest hidden expenses (Boushey & Glynn, 2012).

Work-family conflict exacerbates the crisis. Due to hospitality's 24/7 nature and "face time" culture, work roles frequently interfere with family responsibilities, creating bidirectional conflict (Mesmer-Magnus & Viswesvaran, 2005). Research during COVID-19 found that hospitality work environment significantly increases both work-family conflict and turnover intentions, with work-family conflict partially mediating this relationship (Ahmed & Elsayed, 2022). Female hospitality workers in India reported work-life balance skewed heavily toward work, with only 4% experiencing true equilibrium (CultureMonkey, 2024). The impact extends beyond the workplace. Chronic stress leads to anxiety, depression, high blood pressure, and weakened immune function (Huang et al., 2019). Burned out employees bring diminished capacity to personal relationships, creating family strain that further reduces well-being. The vicious cycle perpetuates as exhausted workers perform poorly, face additional pressure, and consider leaving the industry entirely.

Critically, burnout affects managers as severely as frontline staff. Research found that 76% of hospitality managers experience burnout (Planday, 2024). When leaders responsible for supporting teams are themselves struggling, organizational dysfunction multiplies. Burned out managers lack the emotional resources to coach effectively, recognize employee distress, or model healthy work habits.

Evidence-Based Solutions

Addressing work-life imbalance requires multifaceted interventions targeting both policy and culture. Research identifies several high-impact strategies:

Flexible Scheduling Systems: Implementing self-scheduling or shift bidding technologies allows employees greater control over work hours, significantly improving satisfaction (Celayix, 2024). Rotational shift patterns, compressed workweeks, and advance notice requirements reduce unpredictability. Organizations with formal flexibility policies report 19% lower turnover rates (Lee & Way, 2010).

Wellness Infrastructure: Comprehensive employee well-being programs reduce burnout incidence by 90% (Workhuman, 2023). Effective programs include stress management training, mental health counseling access, peer support groups, and physical wellness resources. Equally important are manager training programs teaching recognition of burnout warning signs and appropriate supportive responses (EHL Hospitality Insights, 2023).

Leadership Modeling: Managers must visibly practice work-life balance, taking breaks, utilizing scheduled time off, and avoiding excessive overtime. When leaders model healthy boundaries, employees feel permission to do likewise (Borzillo, 2023). Regular "wellness check-ins" normalize conversations about workload and stress, creating channels for early intervention before burnout becomes acute.

Systemic Work Design: Organizations must critically examine job design, asking whether current staffing models create inherently unsustainable demands. Adequate staffing levels, realistic performance expectations, and equitable distribution of undesirable shifts all contribute to sustainability (Buick & Thomas, 2001).

Career Development as Retention

Beyond work-life balance, the absence of visible career pathways drives hospitality turnover. Employees frequently perceive the industry as offering limited growth opportunities, pushing ambitious workers to seek advancement elsewhere (Davidson, Timo, & Wang, 2010). Research by Choi and Joung (2017) found that perceived career growth opportunities reduce turnover intentions by 52% among hotel employees, demonstrating the retention power of transparent advancement systems.

- Effective career development frameworks include:
- Clearly defined progression tracks with specific competency requirements
- Regular career development conversations between managers and employees
- Internal job boards providing visibility into opportunities

- Both vertical advancement and lateral movement options for skill diversification
- Investment in training, certifications, and leadership development programs

Organizations excelling at retention create "career academies" offering structured learning pathways from entry-level positions through management. These systems communicate that the organization invests in employee futures, generating loyalty and reducing the need to exit for growth (Schein, 1978; Super, 1980).

The AI Dimension: Technological Disruption and Imposter Amplification

The rapid integration of artificial intelligence into hospitality operations introduces a new dimension to imposter syndrome. The hospitality AI market, valued at $90 million in 2023, is expanding at 60% annually and projected to exceed $8 billion by 2033 (NetSuite, 2025). This transformation requires managers to develop technological literacy while maintaining the human connection that defines hospitality excellence.

Research by Kumawat et al. (2024) found that AI adoption significantly affects employee well-being, with many workers fearing job displacement despite evidence that AI augments rather than replaces human roles. Managers face dual pressures: learning to leverage AI tools for revenue management, demand forecasting, and operational efficiency while simultaneously coaching anxious team members through technological transitions (Fernandez-Vidal et al., 2022). The skills gap is substantial. Traditional hospitality managers were trained in interpersonal service and operational execution, not data analytics or machine learning applications. When expected to implement AI driven systems, many experience renewed imposter feelings, questioning whether they possess the competencies required for modern leadership (Malone, 2024). A 2025 study of accommodation managers found that while executives recognize AI's strategic importance, they struggle to integrate it into existing systems and train employees effectively (Lee et al., 2025).

The solution lies in reframing AI as a tool that frees managers to focus on distinctly human skills: coaching, relationship building, and creative problem solving. Research consistently shows that successful AI integration depends on complementing technological capabilities with enhanced human elements (Singh & Sharma, 2024). Organizations must provide managers with both technical training in AI applications and reassurance that their leadership value centers on developing people, not operating systems.

The Imperative for Change

The problems examined in this chapter reflect fundamental misalignments between hospitality's operational models and human sustainability. Promoting managers without leadership development, demanding unsustainable work hours, and introducing transformative technologies without adequate support creates a perfect storm of dysfunction. The costs measured in turnover, burnout, reduced service quality, and organizational instability, are no longer acceptable.

The following chapters present an integrated playbook for addressing these challenges through evidence-based interventions. These strategies, grounded in decades of organizational research and hospitality-specific studies, offer pathways toward building resilient, high-performing teams led by confident, competent managers. The industry's future depends on this transformation.

Chapter 3: The Coachable

"The best coaches don't just teach skills. They see something in you that you can't yet see in yourself, and they refuse to let you settle for less than becoming it."

The Desert Sky

I was ten years old when my world split in half.

The first half ended on a Mississippi October afternoon when my parents said, "This is your last week of school." The second half began 7,000 miles away, under a Saudi Arabian sky so vast and strange that I couldn't tell if I was looking up at heaven or down into some infinite mirror. Between these two halves, I stood at an airplane window, watching America disappear beneath the clouds, my grandmother's tears still fresh in my memory, and wondered if I would ever feel at home again.

This is not just a story about a boy who moved to a foreign country. It is a story about what it means to be coachable, that rare quality that separates those who merely occupy space from those who transform it. It is about the precise moment when someone sees potential in you that you cannot see in yourself, and how that moment of recognition can echo through decades, shaping not just a career but an entire philosophy of leadership.

In the hospitality industry, we talk endlessly about "guest experience" and "service excellence," but we rarely name the actual magic we're chasing: the alchemy that happens when one human being makes another human being feel seen, valued, and capable of more. That alchemy doesn't begin with a five-star hotel lobby or a Michelin-starred restaurant. It begins the moment someone recognizes your potential and invites you to step into it.

For me, that moment arrived on a dusty soccer field in the Saudi Arabian desert, delivered by a British coach who would teach me more about leadership in three years than most people learn in a lifetime.

The Country Boy and the Unknown

Life in South Mississippi had been beautifully simple. I played American football with a ferocity that earned me the defensive player of the year award, not because I was the most skilled, but because I loved the collision, the controlled chaos, the way everything became clear in the moment of impact. I worked mornings on a shrimp boat, the nets rough against my ten-year-old hands, the salt air mixing with diesel fumes, feeling grown in a way that only hard work can make you feel. I had just noticed girls for the first time. Amy Engle was her name, a cheerleader whose smile suggested that maybe, just maybe, there was more to life than touchdowns and tackle counts.

I was settling into the rhythm of a Southern childhood when my parents announced we were moving to Saudi Arabia.

At first, no one believed me. My fifth-grade teacher called my parents in for a conference; certain I was fabricating stories. My classmates laughed when I said goodbye at the end of that school year, then mocked me when I returned for the start of sixth grade. "I thought you were moving to Saudi Arabia," they taunted, and I had no defense except the truth: my parents kept saying "soon."

Then October came, and "soon" became "now."

I never got to say goodbye properly. One day I was scraping shrimp boat nets and planning my next football practice; the next, I was unbuckled in the back seat of our car, watching my grandmother cry as we drove away. Her figure grew smaller until she was just a memory, and then we were at an airport, and then we were 35,000 feet above an ocean I'd never crossed, and then I was pressing my face against the airplane window watching the only world I'd ever known dissolve into clouds.

The flight stretched endlessly, hours blurring together as we crossed not just distance but entire ways of being. When we finally descended into Saudi Arabia, the heat hit me through the plane door like a physical wall. The air was different: dry, scorching, tasting of sand and diesel and something ancient I had no name for. Men in white thobes moved through the airport with an unhurried grace. Women in black abayas seemed to float rather than walk. The rhythmic call to prayer echoed from somewhere I couldn't see, a sound both beautiful and utterly foreign.

Everything I knew about the world was completely wrong.

The Night Drive to Nowhere

Our driver was British, crisp and kind, navigating the desert highway toward a place called Udhailiyah with the casual confidence of someone for whom the impossible had become routine. The landscape outside my window was biblical in its starkness: endless sand, the occasional cluster of palm trees, and every few miles, massive flares of fire rising from the desert floor into the indigo sky.

"What are the fires for?" I asked, leaning between the two front seats.

"That's how they burn off the gas," the driver said simply, as if this explained everything.

I pressed my face against the window and watched the horizon. Everywhere I looked, flames reached toward a sky crowded with stars brighter than any I'd seen in Mississippi. The desert was burning and beautiful and terrifying, and I was being driven into its heart by a stranger with a gentle accent who was patiently explaining to my parents the rules of a world I didn't understand.

"Football?" the driver asked me, making conversation. "You play?"

"Yes sir," I said. "Defensive player of the year."

He smiled. "Football? We have that here too. You should come to the field tomorrow afternoon."

I didn't know yet that he was talking about soccer. I didn't know that tomorrow I would meet a man who would change the entire trajectory of my life. I didn't know that within weeks, I would discover that being coachable is not the same as being obedient, and that true hospitality is not about making people comfortable but about making them capable.

All I knew was that I was ten years old, 7,000 miles from everything familiar, and someone had just offered me a way forward.

Coach Scott and the Red Clay Field

The next afternoon, jet-lagged and disoriented, I found my way to the soccer field. It was nothing like the manicured football fields of Mississippi. The ground was red clay mixed with sand, hard-packed and dusty, surrounded by a chain-link fence and a handful of weathered bleachers. In the distance, the endless desert stretched toward mountains that shimmered in the heat like mirages.

Coach Scott was standing at midfield, clipboard in hand, whistle around his neck, watching a group of boys run drills. He was British, maybe in his forties, with the bearing of someone who had coached a thousand players and forgotten none of them. When he saw me hovering at the fence, he waved me over.

"You the American boy?" he asked.

"Yes sir."

"Ever played football?"

"Yes sir. Just not this kind."

He smiled. Not a patronizing smile, but the smile of someone who recognized a familiar challenge. "Well then, let's see what you've got."

What I had, it turned out, was aggression without strategy, strength without finesse, and the American football player's instinct to treat every play as a controlled collision. I ran at the ball like I was defending a goal line. I tackled with my whole body. I played with the controlled fury that had made me defensive player of the year, and within ten minutes, Coach Scott pulled me aside.

"Son," he said, not unkindly, "you're playing the wrong game."

I didn't understand. I was trying as hard as I could.

"Soccer isn't about trying hard," he continued. "It's about thinking ahead. It's about reading the field. It's about knowing where the ball is going before it gets there." He paused, making sure I was really listening. "You've got potential. Real potential. But you need to learn to control that aggression. You need to turn that power into precision."

Something shifted in that moment. Not immediately, not like a light switch, but like the first subtle crack in ice that will eventually break apart and reveal the water beneath. For the first time in my young life, someone was seeing not just what I was, but what I could become. And more than that: they were inviting me to see it too.

That invitation, I would later understand, is the essence of being coachable. It is the willingness to accept that someone else might see your potential more clearly than you do. It is humility to admit that strength without strategy is just chaos. It is the courage to let someone reshape you into something better than what you thought possible.

What Makes Someone Coachable?

In the years since that first conversation with Coach Scott, I have spent thousands of hours thinking about what it means to be coachable. As an HR Director in the hospitality industry, I have hired hundreds of people, promoted dozens into management, and watched the painful pattern of talented people failing not because they lacked ability, but because they lacked coachability.

Research confirms what I learned on that red clay field: coachability is the single greatest predictor of long-term success in service industries (Ellinger et al., 2003). It is not about compliance or obedience. It is about receptivity to growth. Studies show that employees who demonstrate high coachability show 32% greater performance improvement over time compared to those with fixed mindsets (Dweck, 2006). In hospitality specifically, where interpersonal skills and adaptability are paramount, coachability becomes not just an advantage but a necessity (Goleman, 1995).

But what exactly makes someone coachable? After decades of observation and experience, I have identified five essential qualities:

1. Self-Awareness Without Self-Judgment

Coachable people can look honestly at their gaps without shame. When Coach Scott told me I was playing the wrong game, I didn't get defensive. I got curious. I wanted to know what he saw that I didn't. This capacity for honest self-assessment, what psychologists call "metacognition," is foundational to all learning (Schön, 1983). Research by Goleman (1995) demonstrates that emotional intelligence begins with self-awareness, the ability to observe your own thoughts, emotions, and behaviors without immediately defending them.

In hospitality, this translates directly to service excellence. A coachable employee who receives feedback about their tone with guests doesn't make excuses; they ask questions. "What did it sound like to you? How could I have said it differently?" They treat feedback not as criticism but as data, and they use that data to improve.

2. Hunger That Outweighs Ego

I wanted to be better at soccer, more than I wanted to be right about how to play it. That hunger created space for Coach Scott's wisdom to enter. Carol Dweck's research on growth mindset demonstrates that individuals who believe abilities can be developed through dedication show significantly higher achievement than those with fixed mindsets (Dweck, 2006). The coachable person says, "I don't know, but I want to learn." The Uncoachable person says, "That's not how we did it at my last job."

In twenty years of hiring, I have learned to screen for hunger. I ask candidates: "Tell me about a time someone's feedback completely changed how you approached your work." The coachable ones light up. The Uncoachable ones get uncomfortable. The difference is not about skill level; it's about whether ego or growth drives their decisions.

3. Pattern Recognition Across Contexts

Coach Scott didn't just teach me soccer. He taught me to think strategically, to read situations before they unfold, to understand that every system has patterns you can learn and leverage. The principles he taught on the field about anticipation, positioning, and teamwork applied everywhere: in school, in relationships, in my eventual career.

Research on transfer learning shows that coachable individuals excel at abstracting lessons from one context and applying them to another (Bransford & Schwartz, 1999). They see connections. When I teach a manager how to give feedback to one difficult employee, the coachable manager asks, "Is this the same approach I should use with my entire team?" They're not just solving the immediate problem; they're building a mental model they can use forever.

4. Comfort with Temporary Incompetence

Learning requires being bad at something before you're good at it. For those first months on the soccer field, I was terrible. I had the wrong reflexes, the wrong instincts, the wrong entire approach to the game. It was humbling. It was frustrating. And it was necessary.

Research on skill acquisition demonstrates that the "learning zone" exists precisely in that space between comfort and panic, where we're challenged enough to grow but not so overwhelmed we shut down (Vygotsky, 1978). Coachable people are willing to be uncomfortable. They understand that the awkwardness of learning is not a sign of failure but evidence of growth.

In hospitality, this is critical. A front desk agent learning a new property management system will make mistakes. A new server will forget orders. A manager learning to give difficult feedback will fumble their words. The coachable ones push through the discomfort. The Uncoachable ones blame the system, the training, or the guests.

5. Trust That the Coach Has Your Best Interest at Heart

This might be the most crucial element of all. I trusted Coach Scott because I could feel that he saw something in me worth developing. His feedback didn't feel like criticism; it felt like investment. Research on coaching effectiveness consistently shows that trust is the foundation of all developmental relationships (Hamlin, Ellinger, & Beattie, 2006). Without trust, feedback feels like attack. With trust, feedback feels like gift.

The best coaches in hospitality create this trust by being consistent, being fair, and being genuinely invested in their people's growth. They remember that every coaching conversation is simultaneously a teaching moment and a hospitality moment. How you make someone feel during feedback determines not just whether they'll implement the feedback, but whether they'll remain coachable over time.

Transformation

Under Coach Scott's guidance, I transformed. Not quickly. Not easily. But steadily, like water reshaping stone.

He taught me to read the field the way a chess master reads a board, seeing not just the current position but three moves ahead. He taught me that strategy beats strength, that patience beats aggression, that a well-timed pass is worth more than a spectacular solo play. He taught me that the best players make everyone around them better, that leadership is not about dominating but about elevating.

More importantly, he taught me to see myself through the lens of potential rather than limitation.

When I looked at my aggressive playing style, I saw a problem that needed fixing. When Coach Scott looked at it, he saw raw material waiting to be shaped. "Channel that energy," he'd say during our one-on-one sessions after practice. "Don't eliminate it. Transform it. Your intensity is your gift. Now we just need to teach you when to use it and when to hold it back."

This reframing changed everything. I wasn't broken and in need of repair. I was incomplete and in the process of becoming. The difference between those two perspectives is the difference between shame and possibility, between shrinking and expanding, between giving up and showing up.

The lessons extended far beyond the red clay field. Our team traveled across Saudi Arabia, playing in remote camps where the fields were nothing more than patches of sand marked with makeshift goals, and in bustling towns like Hofuf and Abqaiq where stands filled with enthusiastic crowds who chanted in Arabic and clapped rhythms I was still learning to understand.

Often, I was the only American on the team bus. I'd put on my headphones, let Journey's "Don't Stop Believin'" wash over me, and stare out at the endless desert landscape, thinking about how far I'd come from Mississippi and how much further I still had to go. The desert became a kind of meditation: unchanging yet always different depending on the light, the time of day, and the season. It taught me that transformation is like that too. You're still fundamentally yourself, but the way you show up in the world shifts completely.

Each trip taught me adaptability. Each match against unfamiliar teams taught me to read new patterns quickly. Each victory taught me humility. Each loss taught me resilience. And through it all, Coach Scott was there, not hovering or micromanaging, but observing, guiding, believing.

He never let me settle. He never let me make excuses. And he never, not once, stopped believing that I could be better than I was the day before.

That belief was its own kind of hospitality. He was making space for me to become.

The Melting Pot

My school in Udhailiyah was a beautiful chaos of cultures. The classrooms held Canadian kids with their "ehs" and hockey references, British kids with their crisp accents and dry humor, South American kids with their effortless cool and rapid-fire Spanish, Indian kids with their multiple languages and different festivals, and me, the lone American kid trying to figure out where I fit in this global puzzle.

At first, the diversity overwhelmed me. Everyone seemed to know things I didn't, spoke languages I couldn't understand, referenced customs and histories I'd never encountered. But slowly, something remarkable happened: I realized that we were all expatriate children, all displaced, all trying to find our place in this Arabian desert that wasn't home to any of us.

We formed friendships not despite our differences but because of them. During lunch, we'd gather in circles and share stories of our home countries. The British kids would talk about rainy London and proper tea. The South American kids would describe beaches and festivals I could barely imagine. The Indian kids would explain Diwali and teach us Hindi phrases that made us laugh when we mispronounced them.

These lunch conversations became my education in a truth that would shape my entire career in hospitality: people from radically different backgrounds can share the same dreams, fears, and aspirations. The surface differences that seem so significant fade when you're willing to see humanity underneath.

One afternoon, during a particularly intense lunch debate about which country had the best food, a Canadian kid named Marcus said something I've never forgotten: "Maybe it's not about which is best. Maybe it's about how much better everything gets when we share it all."

He was talking about food. But he was also talking about something much larger: the abundance that comes from diversity, the richness that emerges when different perspectives collide and create something new.

This, I would later understand, is the essence of hospitality culture. Not homogeneity, not everyone thinking and acting the same way, but a deliberate cultivation of diversity held together by shared values and mutual respect.

Our camp, Udhailiyah, became a microcosm of this principle. It was a small community in the middle of nowhere, thrown together by circumstance, forced to make something work despite our differences. And we did. Not perfectly, not without friction, but we did it. We created a place that felt like home even though it was temporary, even though we all knew we'd eventually leave, even though none of us belonged there originally.

That's hospitality too: making home out of the temporarily, creating belongings where none existed before, building community from strangers.

The Desert Lessons

As I continued to play soccer, traveling across Saudi Arabia with my team, I developed a deep appreciation for the sport and its emphasis on teamwork, strategy, and leadership. But more than that, I developed an appreciation for the way the desert taught lessons without speaking.

The desert doesn't negotiate. It doesn't make exceptions. It simply is, in all, its harsh beauty and unforgiving clarity. You adapt to it, or you suffer. You respect it or it breaks you. You learn to read its signs, or you get lost.

On long bus rides between matches, I'd watch the landscape and think about how similar the desert was to the hospitality industry I would eventually enter. Both demand constant adaptation. Both punish those who can't read patterns and anticipate changes. Both require you to find beauty in repetition, to make the mundane feel special, to create oases of comfort in otherwise harsh environments.

The way the desert transforms with light became a metaphor I didn't know I was learning. At noon, the desert is brutal, all harsh angles and blinding brightness. But at dawn and dusk, it becomes ethereal, the sand turning gold and pink and purple, the whole world softening into something almost tender. Same desert. Different light. Completely different experiences.

That's hospitality too. The hotel is the same building whether it's noon or midnight, but the experience you create can be completely different depending on how you illuminate it, how you frame it, how you guide guests through it.

My time in Saudi Arabia also exposed me to the concept of hospitality in its purest, most cultural form. The Arab tradition of hospitality is ancient and sacred. Guests are treated not as customers but as gifts. Welcoming strangers is not just good business; it's a moral imperative, a spiritual practice.

I watched how the local people approached hospitality: the way they insisted on serving tea even when they had little to offer, the way they made space in their homes for visitors, the way they treated generosity not as transaction but as honor. There was no calculation in it, no wondering what they'd get in return. The act of welcoming itself was the point.

This contrasted sharply with the transactional hospitality I would later encounter in American hotels and restaurants, where every smile was measured, every gesture calculated for maximum tip or review score. The Saudi approach taught me that true hospitality comes from a place of abundance, not scarcity. You give because you have, not because you expect something back.

These values seeped into my understanding of what I wanted my career to be about. I didn't want to just run efficient operations or hit service metrics. I wanted to create spaces where people felt genuinely welcomed, seen, and cared for. I wanted to build teams that operated from abundance rather than scarcity, from generosity rather than calculation.

Return and Recognition

After ninth grade, the realities of American high school pulled me back to the States. The transition was easier than I expected, not because I'd forgotten Saudi Arabia, but because the experiences there had fundamentally changed how I approached everything.

The discipline and strategic thinking I'd developed under Coach Scott's guidance served me well, not just in soccer but in school, in relationships, in navigating the social hierarchies of American teenagers. I could read patterns now. I could anticipate. I could position myself strategically rather than just reacting emotionally.

I played soccer through high school with a level of skill and understanding that surprised my American coaches. They'd ask where I learned to read the field so well, and I'd tell them about Coach Scott and the red clay field in the Saudi Arabian desert, and they'd nod politely but I could tell they didn't quite understand what I was trying to say.

How do you explain that a British coach in a desert taught you not just soccer but an entire philosophy of growth? How do you convey that the lessons weren't really about sport at all, but about learning to see yourself as constantly becoming rather than already being?

My passion for soccer and the strategic foundation Coach Scott had built led me to compete in the Junior Olympics, a prestigious event showcasing the nation's best young talent. Standing on that field, competing against players who'd trained their entire lives in elite American soccer academies, I held my own not because I was the strongest or fastest, but because I knew how to read the game, anticipate plays, and work within team structures.

During one crucial match, facing a team from California with players twice my size, I found myself in a familiar pattern: the urge to play aggressively, to prove myself through force. But then I heard Coach Scott's voice in my head: "Channel it. Transform it. Use your intensity strategically."

I positioned myself not where the ball was, but where I knew it would be three passes from now. I communicated constantly with my teammates, reading their movements, anticipating their needs. When the moment came, I was exactly where I needed to be. The pass came. I controlled it. I passed it forward to a teammate in a better position. He scored.

That goal wasn't mine statistically, but it was mine strategically. And in that moment, I understood what Coach Scott had been trying to teach me all along: that the best players make everyone around them better, that true success is measured not by individual glory but by team elevation, that leadership is about creating opportunities for others to shine.

After the match, one of the opposing team's coaches approached me. "Where'd you learn to play like that?" he asked. "You don't play like an American kid."

I smiled, thinking about red clay fields and desert sunsets and a British coach who saw potential in an aggressive football player and patiently shaped it into something more beautiful.

"Saudi Arabia," I said. "I learned to play in Saudi Arabia."

The Heart of Hospitality

If you remember nothing else from this chapter, remember this: hospitality at its deepest level is about making people feel capable of more than they thought possible.

It's not just about a comfortable bed, though that matters. It's not just about a perfectly mixed cocktail, though that matters too. It's not just about a warm greeting at the front desk, though warmth matters always.

It's about the moment when someone feels seen not just for who they are, but for who they could become.

When a guest walks into your hotel exhausted from travel, overwhelmed by life, carrying invisible burdens you'll never know about, you have a choice. You can process their check-in efficiently, or you can see them. You can notice the exhaustion, read the subtle signs of stress, and create a moment of relief they didn't know was possible.

That's hospitality.

When an employee makes a mistake, revealing a gap in their knowledge or judgment, you have a choice. You can correct the error and move on, or you can develop the person. You can point out what went wrong, or you can help them see the pattern underneath the mistake and coach them toward better judgment next time.

That's leadership.

When someone joins your team uncertain and nervous, bringing potential you can see but they can't, you have a choice. You can give them a handbook and a training schedule and wish them luck, or you can believe in them loudly enough that they start believing in themselves.

That's coaching.

These aren't different skills. They're all the same skill, applied in different contexts. It's the skill Coach Scott taught me on a dusty soccer field in Saudi Arabia when I was ten years old and didn't know who I was or what I could become.

He saw an aggressive American football player and recognized that underneath the aggression was passion, and underneath the passion was potential. He didn't try to eliminate who I was. He helped me transform it into something more useful, more strategic, more beautiful.

That's what great hospitality does. That's what great coaching does. That's what great leadership does.

It sees people not as they are, but as they could be. And then it creates the conditions for that transformation to unfold.

The Coachable Spirit in Practice

To be coachable is to live with radical openness to becoming. It's to understand that you are not a finished product but a work in progress, that feedback is fertilizer for growth, that the discomfort of learning is the price of evolution.

It's to trust that somewhere, right now, there is a Coach Scott for you: someone who sees your potential more clearly than you see it yourself, someone who will push you past what you thought possible, someone who will refuse to let you settle for good enough when great is within reach.

And here's the beautiful paradox: the more coachable you become, the more capable you are of coaching others. Because coaching is not about having all the answers. It's about asking the right questions. It's about seeing clearly. It's about believing in potential so fiercely that your belief becomes contagious.

In my career in hospitality, I've seen this pattern repeat endlessly. The managers who thrive are not necessarily the most talented or experienced when they start. They're the most coachable. They're the ones who can hear "You're doing this wrong" and translate it into "I have room to grow." They're the ones who treat every challenge as a learning opportunity, every failure as valuable data, every piece of feedback as a gift.

And most importantly, they're the ones who extend that same coaching mindset to their teams. They create cultures where people feel safe being imperfect, where growth is celebrated more than perfection, where potential matters more than resume.

I think about the front desk agent I hired years ago, let's call her Maria, who was technically competent but emotionally flat. She checked guests in efficiently but without warmth. She solved problems correctly but without empathy. On paper, she was doing everything right. In practice, she was missing the entire point of hospitality.

I could have corrected her: "Smile more. Be warmer. Show more personality." That's management.

Instead, I coached her: "When you check someone in, what are you paying attention to?" She listed the technical steps. "What about the person in front of you? What do you notice about them?" She looked confused. "Try this: before you say anything, take a breath and really look at the person. See them. Then welcome them like you're genuinely glad they're here."

The shift was subtle but profound. She started noticing that business travelers were often stressed. Families were often tired. Solo travelers were often lonely. And once she saw them, really saw them, her entire approach changed. The warmth wasn't forced; it was natural, emerging from genuine recognition of the human being in front of her.

A year later, Maria was training new employees, and I overheard her telling them: "Don't just check people in. See them first. Everything else follows from that."

She had become coachable, and in becoming coachable, she'd become a coach.

The Legacy of Coach Scott

I never saw Coach Scott again after I left Saudi Arabia. We didn't have social media then, no easy way to stay connected across continents. I've searched for him over the years, wondering where he is, what he's doing, whether he knows the impact he has had.

But in another way, I see him every day. I see him in every manager I coach through a difficult transition. I see him in every employee who struggles at first but is willing to learn. I see him in every moment when I choose to see potential rather than limitation, possibility rather than problem.

His legacy isn't in trophies or championships. It's in the hundreds of people I've coached over the decades, who've gone on to coach hundreds more, creating ripples that extend far beyond that red clay field in the Arabian desert.

That's the thing about true coaching, true hospitality, true leadership: it's fractal. It replicates itself. When you help someone become more than they thought possible, they go out into the world and help others do the same. The gifts multiply.

Coach Scott taught me soccer, but more importantly, he taught me how to see people. He taught me that potential is everywhere, waiting to be recognized and nurtured. He taught me that the greatest gift you can give someone is belief in their becoming.

And now, thirty-five years later, standing in hotel lobbies and conference rooms, coaching managers through the same kind of transformation I experienced, I'm still carrying forward what he started on that dusty field.

I'm still saying, in my own way, what he said to me: "You've got potential. Real potential. Now let's work together to help you see it."

The Invitation

This part of the chapter is not just my story. It's an invitation.

An invitation to see yourself as coachable, regardless of where you are in your career, regardless of how much you think you already know, regardless of how comfortable or uncomfortable growth feels right now.

An invitation to see your team as coachable, to look past the mistakes and the gaps and the frustrations and see the potential waiting to be developed.

An invitation to see hospitality itself as coaching: the practice of making people feel not just comfortable but capable, not just served but seen, not just welcomed but transformed.

In the chapters that follow, we'll explore specific plays for building coachable teams, developing coachable leaders, and creating organizational cultures where growth is not just encouraged but expected. We'll get tactical and practical and specific.

But everything we discuss will rest on this foundation: that hospitality, in its essence, is the practice of seeing and developing potential in others.

It's what Coach Scott did for me on a red clay field in the Arabian desert.

It's what the best hospitality leaders do for their teams every single day.

And it's what you can learn to do, if you're willing to embrace the coachable spirit.

Because in the end, the question is not whether you have potential. You do. We all do.

The question is whether you're willing to be seen, to be shaped, to be challenged, and to be transformed by someone who believes in your becoming.

That's what it means to be coachable.

And it changes everything.

A Final Memory

I'm standing in a luxury hotel in Arizona, watching a new front desk agent fumble through her first solo check-in. She's nervous, apologizing too much, forgetting steps. The guest is patient but tired. The moment is uncomfortable.

I caught her eye and smile. Not a corrective smile, but a believing smile. After the guest leaves, I pull her aside.

"How'd it feel?" I ask.

"Terrible," she says. "I messed everything up."

"What did you learn?"

She pauses, surprised by the question. "I... I think I was so worried about the steps that I forgot about the person."

"Exactly," I say. "You've got potential. Real potential. Now let's work on seeing the person first and letting the steps follow naturally."

Her shoulders relax. She's still nervous, but something has shifted. She's not broken. She's becoming.

Somewhere, 7,000 miles and three decades away, I imagine Coach Scott smiling.

The lesson continues. The transformation ripples forward.

And somewhere, someone else is about to discover what it means to be coachable.

Chapter 4: The Playbook

Every winning coach knows this truth: games aren't won by accident. They're won by preparation, by having the right play for the right moment, by knowing your team so well you can call an audible when the pressures are on. A playbook isn't just a binder full of diagrams. It's the difference between chaos and championship.

In hospitality, we face the same reality. You're coaching a team in an industry where turnover bleeds talent, where burnout lurks behind every double shift, where one bad day can send your best server walking out the door. You need more than good intentions. You need a playbook.

The Hospitality Playbook is that guide: a collection of proven plays designed to strengthen your team, boost employee satisfaction, and stop the revolving door of turnover. But here's what makes this different: this isn't theory from someone who's never worked on a Friday night dinner rush. These plays come from the trenches, from years of leading teams through the beautiful chaos of hospitality, and from lessons learned on playing fields that taught me what it really means to build something that lasts.

A Playbook You Can Actually Use

This book is built for action. Each play connects to online tools you can use immediately: culture assessment checklists, feedback templates, career development worksheets. These resources turn strategy into reality. No more reading about what you should do and wondering how to do it. The tools are there, ready to deploy with your team tomorrow morning.

Throughout these pages, I've woven in personal reflections from my own journey: stories from the field, lessons from coaches who shaped me, moments of failure that became foundations for success. These aren't just anecdotes; they're the connective tissue between coaching philosophy and hospitality leadership. They're proof that the principles that build winning teams work whether you're on a field or behind a host stand.

The Five Plays That Change Everything

The Culture Play: Build the Foundation

Walk into any restaurant, hotel, or venue, and you'll feel it within thirty seconds. Culture isn't what you say in staff meetings. It's what happens when you're not in the room. It's how your team talks to each other during a rush, how they handle mistakes, whether they cover for each other or leave each other hanging.

In hospitality, culture is everything. It's what makes employees show up when they're tired, go the extra mile for a difficult guest, and stay for years instead of months. The Culture Play gives you the framework to build and protect an environment where people don't just work; they belong. You'll learn how to define your core values in ways that matter, how to hire for cultural fit without sacrificing diversity, and how to create rituals and practices that reinforce what you stand for every single day.

When culture is strong, everything else gets easier. When it's weak, nothing else matters.

The Leadership Play: Lead Like You Mean It

Here's the hard truth about hospitality management: you're making fifty decisions before lunch, each one affecting real people with real lives. Your front desk agent who just got snapped at by a guest. Your line cooks who's thinking about quitting. Your new hire who's wondering if they made a mistake taking this job.

Leadership in our industry isn't about barking orders from the office. It's about being present, reading the room, knowing when to push and when to support. The Leadership Play breaks down what it means to lead with empathy without losing standards, to build trust without being everyone's friend, to make tough calls while keeping your team's respect.

You'll explore your own leadership style, strengthen your emotional intelligence, and learn to create an atmosphere where your team doesn't just follow you; they believe in what you're building together. Because great leadership isn't about commanding; it's about inspiring people to bring their best even when things get hard.

The Feedback Play: Make Growth Everyone's Game

Athletes live on feedback. Every practice, every game, every film session: they're constantly learning what works, what doesn't, and how to get better. Yet in hospitality, feedback often becomes the thing everyone dreads annual reviews that feel like ambushes, corrections that sting instead of inspiring, silence when someone's doing great work.

The Feedback Play transforms feedback from a twice a year obligation into the daily rhythm of excellence. You'll learn how to deliver feedback that's specific enough to be useful and positive enough to be motivating. How to create a rich feedback environment where coaching happens naturally, not formally. How to help your team see feedback as fuel for growth, not criticism to endure.

With practical tools for tracking progress and frameworks for difficult conversations, this play ensures feedback becomes your secret weapon for building confidence, competence, and commitment across your entire team.

The Career Path Play: Give Them a Reason to Stay

Here's what keeps talented people leaving hospitality: they can't see a future. They look around and see the same job they're doing now, just five years from now, maybe a dollar more an hour.

No wonder they leave for industries that promise growth.

The Career Path Play tackles hospitality's biggest retention challenge head on. You'll learn how to design clear, achievable career trajectories that inspire ambition instead of resignation. How to identify and develop your rising stars before competitors steal them away. How to create mentorship programs that build loyalty and skills simultaneously.

This play includes skill assessment tools, goal setting templates, and development frameworks that help employees see not just their next step, but the path that leads to their dreams. When your team can envision their future in your organization, they stop looking elsewhere. They invest. They stay. They grow.

The Inclusion Play: Harness the Power of Difference

The best teams in sports aren't made of identical players; they're built from diverse strengths working in harmony. Different perspectives, different skills, different backgrounds all contributing to something none of them could achieve alone. Hospitality works the same way, only better, because our strength is diverse. Our guests come from everywhere, speak different languages, and have different needs. How can we serve them well if our teams don't reflect that reality?

The Inclusion Play gives you the roadmap for building a team where everyone belongs. You'll learn how to spot unconscious bias in hiring, how to create psychological safety where people share ideas freely, how to celebrate differences while building unity. From inclusive hiring practices to equity in advancement opportunities, this play provides both the philosophy and the practical steps to make inclusion more than a buzzword; to make it your competitive advantage.

How the Plays Work Together

Here's what I learned from decades in sports and hospitality: there's no silver bullet. No single play wins the game. It's how the plays work together, how they reinforce each other, how they create something bigger than the sum of their parts.

Strong culture needs authentic leadership. Effective feedback requires clear career paths. Inclusion strengthens culture. Leadership drives inclusion. They're interconnected, each one supporting and amplifying the others. That's why this playbook doesn't give you one solution; it gives you a system.

As you work through each play, you'll see how they build on each other. How a culture of belonging makes feedback easier. How clear career paths reinforce your leadership credibility. How inclusion initiatives strengthen team bonds. This isn't a linear process; it's an ecosystem where every improvement creates ripples that strengthen everything else.

Your Coaching Journey Starts Here

Approach this playbook like a coach preparing for the season. Study each play but stay ready to adapt. Your team is unique: different personalities, different challenges, different opportunities. The strategies here are proven, but they're not rigid. Make them yours. Adjust them to fit your reality. The online tools give you flexibility to customize your approach, so every play becomes a living part of your leadership practice.

Throughout these chapters, you'll find stories from my own journey: the wins, the losses, the moments that taught me what really matters. Leadership isn't something you master and check off. It's a constant evolution, shaped by every team you lead, every challenge you face, every person you help develop. These reflections are reminders that we're all learning, all growing, all finding our way forward.

The Game Plan

In the chapters ahead, we'll break down each play in detail. You'll get the theory that explains why it works, the practical steps to implement it, and the tools to make it stick. You'll see real examples, avoid common pitfalls, and learn how to measure your progress.

Whether you're running your first shift or your thousandth, whether you're managing a small café or a massive resort, this playbook meets you where you are and gives you what you need to get better. Not perfect. Better. Because that's what great coaches do: they make their teams better every single day.

So, here's my challenge to you: approach each play with intensity. With curiosity. With the commitment to do something different than what got you here. Because your team is watching, learning from you, deciding whether to invest their energy and talent in what you're building.

You've got the playbook. You've got talent on your roster. Now it's time to run the plays that turn potential into performance, that transform good teams into great ones, that make hospitality not just a job, but a calling worth staying for.

Let's get to work.

Play #1 Cultural Play

A Story of a Personal Mission

Coach Scott was more than just a soccer coach. He was a mentor, a guide, a beacon of wisdom during my formative years in Saudi Arabia. On one particularly scorching practice session under the relentless desert sun, he taught me one of the most profound lessons of my life: the importance of a personal mission.

"Alright, everyone, gather around!"

Coach Scott's voice boomed across the field as he motioned for the team to bring it in. The heat was merciless. Sweat poured down our faces, stinging our eyes, but there was something about his commanding presence that always captured our attention. We formed a tight circle around him, heavily breathing and shuffling feet creating hushed anticipation.

He looked at each of us, his expression dead serious.

"Today, we're not just going to talk about soccer," he began, his voice steady and calm. "We're going to talk about life and what drives you, both on and off the field."

I leaned in. Coach Scott often integrated life lessons into training, but this felt different. There was an intensity in his eyes that demanded we listen.

"Each of you has a mission," he continued. "Not just as players, but as individuals. And it's critical that you know what that mission is. It's the foundation upon which you'll build your life."

He paused, letting his words sink deep into the blistering afternoon.

"I want each of you to think about your personal mission. It should be something that defines who you are and what you stand for."

I had never thought about having a personal mission before. That seemed like something reserved for adults or corporations, not for a kid like me. But as Coach Scott spoke, I began to understand the power of such a declaration.

"Your mission should be simple but profound," he explained. "It should guide your decisions, your actions, and your interactions with others."

Then Coach Scott shared his own personal mission: "To inspire and nurture the human spirit, one person, one play at a time."

Clear. Concise. Deeply meaningful.

"Now, I want each of you to come up with your own mission," he instructed. "Think about what drives you, what you're passionate about, and what values are most important to you."

Finding SOUL

Over the next few days, I wrestled with Coach Scott's challenge. I thought about the qualities I admired most in him and other role models in my life. I considered what made me feel truly alive and what I wanted to achieve in the long run. Slowly, deliberately, a word began to form in my mind. A word that encapsulated everything I aspired to be.

One afternoon, as the sun began to set and cast long shadows across the practice field, I approached Coach Scott with my mission statement. He was sitting in the stands, his gaze fixed on the empty field, lost in thought.

"Coach," I called out, breaking his concentration. "I think I've got it."

He turned to me with a smile and motioned for me to sit beside him. "Let's hear it."

I took a deep breath. "My mission is one word: SOUL."

Coach Scott raised an eyebrow, intrigued. "SOUL?"

I nodded, the word feeling powerful in my mouth. "It stands for Strong Integrity, Overwhelming Passion, Understanding of oneself, and Lasting commitment."

A slow smile spread across his face. "I like that. Tell me more."

I explained how each element of SOUL represented a key aspect of who I was. Strong Integrity meant always doing the right thing, even when it was difficult. Overwhelming Passion was about putting my heart and soul into everything I did. Understanding of oneself meant knowing my strengths and weaknesses and being true to who I was. And Lasting commitment represented my dedication to my goals and the people I cared about.

Coach Scott listened intently, nodding as I spoke. When I finished, he placed a hand on my shoulder.

"That's a powerful mission," he said. "If you live by those principles, you'll be able to handle anything that comes your way."

From that day forward, SOUL became my guiding light. It was more than just a word; it was a philosophy that shaped my actions and decisions. Whether I was on the soccer field, in the classroom, or navigating the challenges of everyday life, I always strived to embody the principles of Strong Integrity, Overwhelming Passion, Understanding of oneself, and Lasting commitment.

This lesson from Coach Scott and the concept of SOUL had a profound impact on my life. It gave me a sense of purpose and direction, providing a foundation upon which I could build my future. No matter where life took me, I knew I had the strength, passion, self-awareness, and commitment to succeed.

Years later, as I embarked on my career in the hospitality industry, the principles of SOUL continued to guide me. I applied the same dedication and integrity to my work, always striving to create an environment where both employees and guests felt valued and inspired. The overwhelming passion I had for soccer translated into a deep love for hospitality and service, and my understanding of myself helped me lead with empathy and authenticity.

Looking back, I realized that Coach Scott's lesson on creating a personal mission was one of the most important teachings of my life. It taught me the power of clarity and focus, and how a single word could encapsulate my core values and aspirations. SOUL wasn't just a mission statement; it was a way of life, and it had positioned me to handle anything that came my way.

Success at the Podium

Visualization is a powerful tool for achieving success. By creating a vivid picture of what winning looks like, you can inspire and motivate your team to work towards that vision with everything they have.

Coach Scott, ever the strategist, knew that the foundation of any successful season lay not just in physical training but in mental preparation as well. To kick off the season on a high note, he decided to host a team party, a gathering that would go beyond the usual pep talks and drills.

We gathered at Coach Scott's house on a Saturday afternoon. His backyard had been transformed into a mini soccer wonderland, with goalposts set up and banners from past seasons hanging proudly. There was electricity in the air as we ran around, sharing stories and aspirations for the upcoming season. But Coach Scott had a different agenda for the day, one that would shape our mindset and approach the game in ways we hadn't anticipated.

After an hour of fun and games, Coach Scott called us in. We formed a circle on the grass, and he stood in the middle, holding a shiny trophy. It wasn't the actual championship trophy, but one from his old playing days, brought out to help us visualize our goal. He placed it on a small table in the center of the circle, its golden surface glinting in the afternoon sunlight.

"Today, I want us to talk about what it means to win," Coach Scott began, his voice calm but charged with purpose. "I want you all to close your eyes for a moment and imagine this trophy is the real deal. Imagine it's the end of the season, and we've just won the championship."

We closed our eyes, and Coach Scott guided us through the visualization.

"Picture yourself holding this trophy. Feel its weight in your hands. Hear the crowd cheering for your name. What do you see? What do you hear? What do you feel?"

In my mind, I saw myself on the field, my teammates around me, all of us beaming with joy. The crowd's roar was deafening, a symphony of applause and cheers. I felt the rough texture of the trophy in my hands; it's cool metal warming under my grip. The sense of accomplishment was overwhelming: a mix of pride, relief, and sheer happiness.

"Now," Coach Scott continued, "think about what you would say at that moment. Who would you thank? What would you reflect on?"

As we envisioned our victory speeches, I thought of my teammates, each one of us contributing to the collective success. I imagined thanking my family for their unwavering support, my teammates for their hard work and trust, and Coach Scott for his guidance and belief in us.

We opened our eyes, and Coach Scott's smile was broad.

"This is what winning feels like," he said. "Hold on to that feeling. Let it drive you through every practice, every game, every challenge. This vision will be our anchor, our motivation. Every time you feel tired or doubtful, remember this moment."

The rest of the party was spent discussing our vision for the season. Coach Scott encouraged us to set specific, measurable objectives, both as a team and individually. We talked about our strengths and weaknesses, the areas we needed to improve, and the strategies we could employ to outplay our opponents.

As the sun set and the party wound down, I realized how powerful the day had been. It wasn't just about envisioning the win; it was about embedding that vision deep within us, making it a part of our daily mindset. Coach Scott had given us a glimpse of what success looked and felt like, and it became a beacon that guided us through the season.

Bringing It in as a Team

In any successful team, whether in sports or business, the foundational element is a unified culture. This culture, or "play," is the underlying force that defines how the team operates, communicates, and supports each other. In hospitality, creating a strong and supportive culture is just as essential as building team unity on the field.

The Culture Play in The Hospitality Playbook offers strategies to help leaders build a positive workplace culture where every team member feels valued, respected, and connected to the organization's mission. By establishing core values, promoting a positive work environment, recognizing achievements, and encouraging ownership, leaders can cultivate an atmosphere where employees feel like integral players rather than replaceable parts.

Establishing Core Values

Core values are the bedrock of any organizational culture. They define what the company stands for and guide decision making at every level. In hospitality, core values might include respect, excellence, teamwork, and integrity.

These values should be more than just words on a wall; they should be lived and breathed by everyone in the organization, from senior leadership to entry level staff.

When I think about core values, I'm reminded of the mission statement I developed as a young soccer player: SOUL. This concept of having a clear, guiding principle applies just as much to organizations as it does to individuals. Leaders need to establish values that resonate with the team and reflect the organization's identity.

To establish core values effectively, involve your team in the process. Ask employees what qualities they believe are important and what values they think the organization should embody. This inclusive approach not only helps identify values that everyone can rally behind but also fosters a sense of ownership and buy in from the start.

Once core values are established, they must be reinforced consistently. Leaders should reference these values in meetings, performance reviews, and day-to-day interactions. They should be woven into the hiring process, training programs, and company policies. When employees see that leadership genuinely lives by these values, they're more likely to adopt them as their own.

Creating a Positive Work Environment

A positive work environment is one where employees feel safe, supported, and motivated to do their best work. This goes beyond physical safety; it includes emotional and psychological well-being. In hospitality, where the pace is fast and stress levels can run high, a positive work environment is essential for retaining talent and maintaining high morale.

Creating this environment starts with leadership. Leaders must be approachable, empathetic, and responsive to their team's needs. An open-door policy, where employees feel comfortable voicing concerns or sharing ideas, can make a significant difference. Regular check ins, whether through one-on-one meetings or team huddles, help leaders stay connected to their team and address issues before they escalate.

Additionally, fostering camaraderie among team members strengthens the work environment. Encourage team building activities, celebrate milestones together, and create opportunities for employees to connect outside of work tasks. In my experience, the best teams are those where members genuinely care about each other's well-being and success.

Physical workspace also matters. Ensure that break rooms are comfortable, that employees have access to proper resources, and that the environment is clean and organized. Small gestures, like providing healthy snacks or creating a quiet space for employees to decompress, can contribute to a more positive atmosphere.

Recognizing and Celebrating Achievements

Recognition is a powerful motivator. When employees feel that their hard work and dedication are noticed and appreciated, they're more likely to remain engaged and committed to the organization. In hospitality, where employees often work long hours and face high pressure situations, regular recognition can make a world of difference. It boosts morale, builds loyalty, and reinforces the values you want to see in your team.

Leaders can use tools such as monthly recognition programs, team shout outs, or a "wall of fame" to highlight outstanding performances. Recognizing achievements is not just about rewarding hard work; it's about reinforcing the behaviors and attitudes that align with the company's values.

In my career, I've seen how a simple "thank you" can go a long way in making employees feel appreciated. When employees feel valued, they're more likely to remain committed to the organization. Regular recognition creates a ripple effect, encouraging others to strive for excellence and feel proud of their contributions. Recognition doesn't always have to be formal or elaborate. Sometimes, a genuine compliment in the moment or a handwritten note can have as much impact as an award ceremony. The key is consistency and sincerity. Employees can tell when recognition is authentic versus when it's just going through the motions.

Encouraging Ownership

One of the most empowering strategies a leader can adopt is to give employees a sense of ownership over their work. In sports, players who take pride in their roles tend to be more dedicated and engaged. In hospitality, this same principle applies. When employees feel that they have control over their responsibilities and the freedom to make decisions, they're more invested in the organization's success.

Encouraging ownership involves entrusting employees with responsibilities and allowing them to make decisions within their role. This can be as simple as giving front line staff the autonomy to handle guest issues or empowering department heads to lead their teams with minimal intervention. By fostering a culture of ownership, leaders signal to employees that they are trusted, valued, and capable.

In my personal journey, I've experienced the impact of ownership firsthand. When I was given the freedom to make decisions and lead projects, my sense of commitment to the organization deepened. Employees who feel a sense of ownership over their work are more likely to stay with the organization, contribute innovative ideas, and take initiative in their roles. It also fosters a sense of accountability, as employees take pride in their contributions to the organization's success.

Ownership also means allowing room for mistakes. When employees know they have the freedom to try new approaches and learn from failures without fear of harsh consequences, they're more likely to innovate and push boundaries. This creates a dynamic, forward-thinking culture where growth is constant.

Strategy for Culture Play

Implementing a culture play in hospitality requires a well-rounded strategy. It starts with leading by example: demonstrating the values you want to see and ensuring they permeate every level of the organization. Leaders should be role models, exemplifying the qualities and values that define the company's culture. One practical approach is to incorporate regular team meetings that not only address operational matters but also focus on the team's overall well-being and development. During these meetings, leaders can check in with team members, discuss any challenges, and celebrate recent successes. Additionally, adopting an open-door policy can encourage employees to approach management with their concerns, fostering an environment of trust and transparency.

Inclusive decision making is another critical element. Employees should feel that their opinions are valued and that they have a say in decisions that affect their roles. This might involve gathering employees input on shift scheduling, inviting team members to contribute ideas for improving guest experiences, or allowing departments to set their own goals. Inclusion creates a sense of ownership and belonging, which is essential to building a positive culture.

In hospitality, culture is not a "set it and forget it" strategy. It requires ongoing attention and consistent reinforcement. Leaders need to be vigilant, continuously assessing the health of the culture and adjusting as needed. Using tools like employee surveys or culture assessments can provide valuable insights into areas for improvement and help ensure that the culture remains strong and aligned with the organization's mission.

Here are some practical steps for implementing the Culture Play:

Define Your Core Values

1. Involve your team in identifying what matters most
2. Make values visible throughout the organization
3. Reference them consistently in meetings and decisions

Create Rituals and Traditions

1. Establish regular team gatherings or celebrations
2. Develop onboarding rituals that welcome new members into the culture
3. Create signature experiences that embody your values

Measure Culture Health

1. Conduct regular employee satisfaction surveys
2. Hold focus groups to gather qualitative feedback
3. Track retention rates and exit interview themes

4. Monitor engagement levels and team dynamics

Reinforce Through Recognition

1. Implement peer to peer recognition programs
2. Celebrate wins publicly and regularly
3. Connect recognition to core values
4. Make appreciation specific and timely

Empower Through Ownership

1. Delegate meaningful responsibilities
2. Give autonomy in decision making
3. Support innovation and calculated risk taking
4. Provide resources and remove obstacles

Personal Reflections: Learning Culture Through SOUL

Reflecting on Coach Scott's influence and my own experiences in hospitality, I'm reminded of how crucial it is to build a strong culture grounded in clear values. The concept of SOUL (Strong Integrity, Overwhelming Passion, Understanding of Oneself, and Lasting commitment) has guided me in my approach to culture building. Just as I learned the importance of having a personal mission, I recognize the value of having a shared mission within a team. A team culture founded on mutual respect, trust, and shared purpose can create a sense of unity that carries the organization through tough times.

Each time I've taken on a leadership role, I've carried these principles with me. Strong integrity ensures that decisions are fair and transparent. Overwhelming passion drives me to create an inspiring work environment. Understanding of oneself allows me to lead with empathy and authenticity, recognizing that each team member brings unique strengths and challenges. Lasting commitment means showing up for my team consistently, through the good times and the difficult seasons.

Culture is not built overnight. It's built through daily actions, through moments of challenge where values are tested, through celebrations where achievements are recognized, and through the quiet consistency of leaders who show up and do what they say they'll do. Just as Coach Scott taught me to have a personal mission, I've learned that organizations need that same clarity of purpose, that same unwavering commitment to what they stand for.

The Culture Play is about creating an environment where people don't just work, they belong. Where they don't just show up, they invest. Where they don't just do their jobs, they contribute to something meaningful. When you get culture right, everything else becomes possible. When culture is weak, nothing else matters.

As you implement the Culture Play in your organization, remember that you're not just building policies and programs. You're building a living, breathing ecosystem where people spend a significant portion of their lives. Make it worth their time. Make it worth their talent. Make it worth their commitment.

Because when culture is strong, teams don't just survive the challenges of hospitality. They thrive. They grow. They become something greater than the sum of their parts.

That's the power of the Culture Play. That's the foundation upon which everything else is built.

Play #2 The Leadership Play

A Personal Journey to Understanding Needs

The Shamal had blown through the night before, coating everything in a fine layer of dust. It was a typical afternoon in Saudi Arabia, the kind where the sun beat down relentlessly and the air felt thick enough to chew. We were halfway through an intense soccer practice when Coach Scott called for a water break.

I made my way to the sidelines where the water jugs were lined up, my throat parched and my muscles screaming. The red dirt clung to my skin, mixing with sweat to create muddy streaks down my arms.

"Take a seat, everyone," Coach Scott said, waving us over to a shaded area. "I want to talk to you about something important."

We gathered around him, grateful for the respite. I could see the curiosity in my teammates' eyes. Coach Scott was known for his impromptu life lessons, and they were always worth hearing.

"Understanding your role on this team is crucial," he began, wiping the sweat from his forehead. "Just like in any organization, every position on the field has specific needs and responsibilities. If we don't understand and fulfill these needs, we won't function as a team, and we certainly won't win any games."

His words struck a chord with me. As a goalkeeper, I knew my role was different from the strikers and midfielders, but I had never considered the broader implications of understanding each position's specific needs. Each player brought something unique to the field. Each position demanded different skills, different mindsets, different preparation.

This wasn't just about soccer.

Coach Scott's lesson stayed with me as I grew older and began my career in hospitality. Just as our soccer team needed to understand the strengths and weaknesses of each player, a hospitality business must analyze its operations to identify staffing needs. I remembered the grueling practices and the meticulous way Coach Scott evaluated each player's performance, ensuring that we were all in the right positions and playing to our strengths.

Leadership, I realized, was about seeing people clearly. Understanding what they needed to succeed. Putting them in positions where they could thrive.

Crafting Detailed Job Descriptions Like a Soccer Team's Playbook

As I look back on my days playing soccer under Coach Scott, the parallels between building a soccer team and creating effective job descriptions in hospitality become strikingly clear. One memory stands out, illustrating the importance of clarity and precision in defining roles.

Coach Scott, always the meticulous planner, decided to introduce a new approach to one season. He gathered us behind the stands, the familiar scent of red dirt and sweat filling the air and handed out neatly bound booklets.

"These," he said, holding up one of the booklets, "are our playbooks for the season."

Curious, we flipped through the pages. Each section meticulously detailed our roles, responsibilities, and the standards we were expected to meet. From the goalkeeper to the forwards, every position was outlined with precision. Coach Scott explained that just like in a job, understanding our specific roles on the field would be key to our success.

"This playbook is not just about tactics and strategies," he explained. "It's about understanding your responsibilities, knowing what's expected of you, and how you fit into the bigger picture of the team."

As a goalie, my role was crucial in communicating with the defense and setting up the attack. The playbook detailed not just my positioning and movements, but also my responsibilities in terms of communication, supporting teammates, and even the standards for my fitness and conduct. It left no room for ambiguity.

Coach Scott's approach was transformative. With each player understanding their specific role, we functioned more cohesively as a unit. There was no confusion about who was supposed to do what, and this clarity translated into our performance on the field. One of the most memorable aspects of Coach Scott's playbook was how it set clear expectations. There was no ambiguity about what was expected from each player, and this clarity was empowering. We knew exactly what we needed to do to succeed, and this knowledge boosted our confidence and performance.

In hospitality, detailed job descriptions serve the same purpose. They eliminate confusion, set clear expectations, and empower employees to excel in their roles. When team members understand exactly what's expected of them, they can focus their energy on execution rather than uncertainty. They can take ownership of their responsibilities and measure their own progress.

A Lesson from the Goalpost

Setting clear expectations and goals for new hires is crucial for aligning their efforts with the overall vision and mission of the organization. Reflecting on my days as a soccer goalie under Coach Scott's guidance, I realized how the principles of setting clear expectations and goals on the field parallel those in hospitality. One season stands out, illustrating how clarity, alignment, and continuous feedback can lead to remarkable success.

It was the beginning of the soccer season, and Coach Scott gathered the team for our first meeting. As the goalie, I knew my role was crucial in defending our goal, but Coach Scott wanted to make sure each player, new and returning, understood their specific roles and how they contributed to the team's overall strategy.

"Today, we're going to do more than just talk tactics," Coach Scott began. "We're going to align our individual goals with our team's vision of winning the championship. Each one of you has a unique role, and it's important to understand how your efforts contribute to our success."

Coach Scott had a clear vision for our team: to be the most formidable defense and the most cohesive unit in the league. He communicated this vision to us, emphasizing that every player's role, from the forwards to the defenders to the goalie, was designed to achieve this objective.

"As the goalie," he said, looking directly at me, "your primary responsibility is to guard our goal. But beyond that, you need to lead the defense, communicate effectively with your teammates, and maintain focus under pressure. Your role is vital in shaping the team's overall strategy."

This clear alignment of my role with the team's vision made me realize the importance of my position not just in preventing goals but in orchestrating the defense and instilling confidence in my teammates. I wasn't just stopping shots; I was the last line of defense and the first line of communication.

To ensure that everyone was on the same page, Coach Scott developed a comprehensive onboarding program for the new players. This included detailed training sessions where experienced players like me mentored the newcomers, sharing insights and strategies specific to our team.

During one of these sessions, I worked closely with a new defender. We practiced drills that simulated game scenarios, focusing on communication and positioning. Coach Scott would often pause the practice to provide feedback, reinforcing our roles and expectations.

"This drill is not just about stopping the ball," he would say. "It's about understanding your position, anticipating the opponent's moves, and working as a unit. Each one of you needs to know not just your role but how it fits into our overall game plan."

Coach Scott believed in setting SMART goals: Specific, Measurable, Achievable, Relevant, and Time bound. For me, this meant not just focusing on the number of saves I made but also improving my reaction time, communication with defenders, and ability to read the game.

"Let's set some goals for the season," Coach Scott said during one meeting. "For you, as the goalie, aim to reduce the number of goals conceded by 20% compared to last season. Work on your reaction drills daily and ensure you coordinate with your defenders to maintain a strong line of defense."

These specific, achievable goals gave me a clear target to aim for and a sense of purpose in my training sessions. Each practice became a step towards achieving these goals, contributing to the team's success. I could measure my progress. I could see improvement. I could feel myself getting better.

Bringing It in as a Team

In sports, effective leadership is the backbone of any successful team. A coach who motivates, guides, and supports players creates a team dynamic that maximizes potential. Similarly, the Leadership Play in hospitality emphasizes leadership skills that inspire, motivate, and support team members. In this play, managers and leaders in hospitality are urged to think like coaches, cultivating a team culture grounded in trust, accountability, and shared purpose.

Leadership, when approached through the lens of a coach, becomes less about authority and more about empowering others to achieve their best. It's about seeing potential where others see only problems. It's about developing talent, not just deploying it.

The Core Elements of Leadership

To understand the essence of this play, let's break down the fundamental components of effective leadership and see how they manifest in both sports and hospitality settings. These principles center around modeling the right behaviors, providing mentorship, empowering team members, and fostering a growth mindset.

Model the Right Behaviors

Just as a coach models discipline and teamwork, managers should demonstrate the behaviors they expect from their team. This ranges from work ethic and commitment to communication style and respect for others. In both sports and hospitality, team members look to their leaders for guidance not only in what they say but in what they do. Modeling the right behavior builds credibility and sets the standard for the rest of the team.

Reflecting on my early years with Coach Scott, I recall one instance that solidified the importance of modeling behavior. We were mid-season, facing a series of tough games that tested our stamina and mental resilience. Coach Scott never faltered. Despite the scorching heat and relentless pressure, he was the first to arrive and the last to leave practice. He ran alongside us during sprints, stayed late to help struggling players, and maintained a level of focus that was infectious.

This relentless commitment showed us that dedication wasn't just expected; it was ingrained in the team culture. His presence on the field, enduring the same grueling practices, made us realize that he wasn't asking us to do anything he wasn't willing to do himself. It was a powerful lesson in how modeling behavior impacts team dynamics.

In hospitality, leaders who model the behaviors they expect create a ripple effect throughout the organization. When a manager treats every guest interaction with care, arrives on time, maintains composure during rushes, and shows respect to every team member regardless of position, they set a standard. Team members notice. They emulate. They internalize these behaviors as the norm rather than the exception.

Provide Mentorship and Development

Great coaches don't just tell players what to do; they invest time in developing each player's skills and understanding of the game. Similarly, effective hospitality leaders act as mentors, guiding team members through challenges, helping them develop professionally, and preparing them for future roles.

Mentorship goes beyond formal training programs. It's about being available, offering guidance in real time, and showing genuine interest in each team member's growth. When leaders take the time to understand individual strengths, weaknesses, and aspirations, they can tailor their approach to help each person reach their potential.

Coach Scott was a master at this. He knew each player's strengths and where they struggled. He would spend extra time after practice working with players who needed additional support, not as punishment but as investment. He saw potential in us that we couldn't always see in ourselves.

In hospitality, mentorship might look like shadowing new employees, providing constructive feedback after challenging situations, or having regular one on one conversations about career goals. Leaders who invest in mentorship create loyalty, build skills, and develop the next generation of leaders within the organization.

Empower Team Members

Empowerment is about giving team members the autonomy to make decisions and take ownership of their roles. In sports, this means trusting players to execute plays, make split second decisions, and adapt to changing game conditions. In hospitality, empowerment means trusting employees to resolve guest issues, make judgment calls, and represent the organization's values in every interaction.

One pivotal lesson in empowerment came when Coach Scott decided to rotate our team captains each week. He wanted each of us to experience leadership, understand its challenges, and grow our confidence. As a goalkeeper, I wasn't the most vocal player but having that temporary leadership role taught me to communicate assertively, trust my instincts, and make decisions that benefited the team.

Empowering each player gave us a sense of ownership, deepened our trust in one another, and helped us appreciate the collective effort it took to succeed. We learned that leadership wasn't about having all the answers; it was about making decisions and standing by them.

In hospitality, empowering employees can have a transformative effect on both the team and guest satisfaction. When team members are trusted to resolve guest issues independently or make adjustments that enhance the guest experience, they feel a greater sense of responsibility and pride in their work. Empowered employees are also more likely to go above and beyond, as they are actively engaged in creating memorable experiences rather than simply following protocols.

Leaders who foster autonomy in their teams help build a culture where initiative and accountability thrive. They create an environment where employees don't need to ask permission for every decision, where they can respond quickly to situations, and where they feel trusted to represent the organization well.

Encourage a Growth Mindset

A winning team embraces growth and improvement. Coaches encourage players to view challenges as opportunities for development, fostering resilience and adaptability. The growth mindset is equally important in hospitality, where each interaction with guests presents an opportunity to learn and grow.

The value of a growth mindset was a concept Coach Scott instilled in us from day one. After every game, win or lose, we would debrief as a team, analyzing our performance and identifying areas for improvement. Coach Scott had a saying: "Every game is a lesson." He encouraged us to see mistakes as learning opportunities rather than failures. This mindset allowed us to bounce back from losses and approach each game with renewed determination.

I remember one particularly tough loss where we'd been outplayed in every aspect of the game. We were dejected, sitting in the locker room in silence. Coach Scott didn't yell or lecture. Instead, he asked us questions. What did we learn? What would we do differently? How could we use this experience to get better?

By framing the loss as data rather than defeat, he helped us extract value from the experience. We weren't failures; we were learners. We weren't done; we were just getting started.

Hospitality leaders can encourage a growth mindset by creating an environment where feedback is valued and learning is prioritized. After busy seasons or challenging events, managers can gather the team to discuss what went well, what could be improved, and how they can collectively enhance their performance. Leaders who emphasize continuous learning and view challenges as growth opportunities empower their teams to approach each day with resilience and adaptability.

Leading with Purpose and Integrity

The Leadership Play is about leading with purpose and integrity, setting the tone for an environment where team members feel valued, motivated, and aligned with organizational goals. Leaders who adopt a coaching mindset prioritize development, feedback, and encouragement. They recognize that their role goes beyond task management; it involves inspiring and fostering potential within each team member.

Effective leadership in hospitality hinges on adaptability, transparency, and accountability. Just as a coach remains agile and responsive to changing dynamics on the field, hospitality leaders must be flexible and ready to adjust to evolving demands in the workplace. Building a successful team requires more than setting objectives; it involves cultivating relationships based on trust and respect, ensuring that team members feel supported in their professional journeys.

Leadership isn't a title; it's a practice. It's what you do every day, in the small moments and the big decisions. It's how you show up when things are going well and how you respond when they're falling apart. It's the consistency of your character and the authenticity of your commitment.

Personal Reflection: Lessons from the Field to the Front Desk

My experiences with Coach Scott not only shaped my understanding of leadership but also provided a foundation for my approach to hospitality. His lessons, whether it was empowering us to take ownership, fostering a growth mindset, or modeling discipline and respect, translated seamlessly into the world of hospitality. I've carried these principles into my roles, striving to create environments where employees feel supported and inspired.

One lesson I carry with me is from a season where our team was struggling. Instead of imposing solutions, Coach Scott gathered us and asked for our thoughts, involving us in the problem-solving process. This inclusion made us feel valued, and it reminded me of the importance of open dialogue in the workplace. When employees are encouraged to share insights and are genuinely heard, they feel a greater sense of connection and investment.

As I moved through various roles in hospitality, I saw firsthand how empowering employees, mentoring them, and fostering a growth mindset could transform team dynamics. Employees who feel respected and valued are more engaged, which translates directly into better guest experience. They bring more energy, more creativity, and more commitment to their work.

Leadership isn't about being the smartest person in the room or having all the answers. It's about creating an environment where the best ideas can emerge, where people feel safe to contribute, and where everyone is working toward a common goal. It's about seeing leadership as service rather than status.

Implementing The Leadership Play: Practical Steps

For hospitality leaders, the Leadership Play offers a practical framework for cultivating strong, resilient teams. It involves setting clear expectations, providing mentorship, empowering autonomy, and fostering continuous growth. Leaders should aim to create a culture where each team member feels they are part of something greater, where their individual efforts contribute to collective success.

Here are some practical ways to implement the Leadership Play in your organization:

Hold Regular Check Ins-Schedule consistent one on one meetings with team members to discuss their goals, challenges, and development opportunities. These shouldn't feel like performance reviews; they should feel like coaching sessions. Ask questions. Listen actively. Understand what each person needs to succeed.

Create Empowerment Programs-Offer training that encourages team members to make decisions confidently and handle guest issues independently. Give them frameworks for decision making, not scripts. Trust them to use their judgment. Celebrate when they take initiative, even if the outcome isn't perfect.

Host Growth Oriented Workshops-Develop workshops focused on resilience, adaptability, and personal development to strengthen the team's growth mindset. Bring in speakers. Share stories of overcoming challenges. Create space for vulnerability and learning. Make development an ongoing conversation, not an annual event.

Model Vulnerability and Learning-Share your own mistakes and what you learned from them. Show your team that growth mindset applies to everyone, including leadership. When you mess up, own it. When you don't know something, admit it. When you're wrong, change course. This modeling gives permission for everyone else to embrace imperfection as part of growth.

Celebrating Effort and Progress-Recognize not just results but the effort, creativity, and resilience people demonstrate. Acknowledge when someone tries something new, takes on a challenge, or helps a teammate. Make growth and development as celebrated as performance metrics.

Provide Clear Pathways for Advancement-Help team members see their future within the organization. Discuss potential career paths. Identify the skills and experiences they need to get there. Create opportunities for them to stretch and grow. Invest in their development as you would in any other critical asset.

The Leadership Commitment-The Leadership Play is more than just a set of principles; it's a commitment to creating an environment where everyone is given the tools, support, and encouragement they need to thrive. By fostering an atmosphere of trust, accountability, and continuous growth, hospitality leaders can build teams that are not only successful in their roles but deeply invested in the organization's mission and values.

Leadership is the bridge between potential and performance. It's what transforms a group of individuals into a cohesive team. It's what turns ordinary service into extraordinary experiences. It's what makes people want to stay, to grow, to give their best. When you lead like a coach, you don't just manage tasks; you develop people. You don't just maintain standards; you raise them. You don't just fill positions; you build careers. You don't just run a business; you create a legacy.

That's the power of the Leadership Play. That's what separates good organizations from great ones. That's what

Coach Scott taught me on dusty fields in Saudi Arabia, and what I've carried into every leadership role since.

Lead with purpose. Lead with integrity. Lead like you mean it.

Because your team is watching, learning, and deciding whether to follow you into the challenges ahead.

Play #3 The Feedback Play

Scouting for Talent

Coach Takes Me on a Fishing Trip

It was a warm, sunny morning when Coach Scott suggested we go on a fishing trip to Half Moon Bay. Half Moon Bay, nestled in the eastern province of Saudi Arabia, offers a picturesque view of the Persian Gulf's tranquil waters. As a young boy who had recently moved to Saudi Arabia from the Mississippi Coast, the prospect of fishing in such an exotic location filled me with excitement and curiosity. I was an expert at fishing; it had been my first job back home.

Little did I know this trip would become one of those life experiences that profoundly shaped my approach to scouting for talent in the hospitality industry.

We packed our gear meticulously, with Coach Scott guiding me through each step.

"Fishing isn't just about throwing a line in the water and hoping for the best," he began as we assembled our rods and tackle. "It's about understanding the environment, knowing where to find the fish, and having the patience to wait for the right moment."

As we set out to walk the jetties, Coach's demeanor shifted from casual to thoughtful. He began to share his wisdom about the art of fishing, emphasizing patience, strategy, and the importance of understanding where to find the best catch. This was not just a casual outing; it was a lesson, a masterclass in the delicate balance between skill and intuition, preparation and adaptability.

"Just like in life and business, you need to know where to look and what to use to attract what you want," he explained.

His words resonated deeply, even if I didn't fully grasp their significance at the time.

We found a spot teeming with fish, and Coach showed me how to cast the line just right and patiently wait for the fish to bite. It was a dance of anticipation and precision, much like finding the right candidate for a job.

As we waited, Coach Scott continued to weave his metaphorical tapestry.

"In talent scouting, identifying the right places to look for candidates and understanding what attracts them is essential," he said. "You have to be prepared, know the right timing, and use the right tools and techniques to increase your chances of success."

We cast our lines, and time seemed to slow down as we waited for the first bite. The gentle lapping of the waves against the rocks and the distant call of seabirds created a serene backdrop for our lesson.

"Think of this as having as many hooks as possible in the sea to catch fish," Coach Scott said, smiling. "The more prepared you are, the better your chances of landing the big one."

Suddenly, my line tugged sharply.

My heart raced as I began to reel in the line, feeling the resistance of a strong fish on the other end. With Coach Scott's guidance, I managed to bring in the biggest fish of the day. It was a moment of triumph and exhilaration, but also one of profound learning.

Coach Scott related this to finding top talent.

"Just as you had to be patient and strategic in fishing, the same principles apply to scouting for talent," he explained. "You need to identify potential candidates, attract them effectively, and ensure you secure the best hires."

The fish flopped around on the jetty, its scales glistening in the sun. Coach Scott's eyes twinkled with a mixture of pride and wisdom.

"Remember this moment," he said. "Knowing where to fish, what bait to use, and how to reel in the best catch are all essential skills. Apply these lessons to your life and your career, and you'll find success."

From Fishing Lines to Talent Pipelines

Over the years, as I transitioned from the soccer field to the hospitality industry, these lessons stayed with me. I found myself drawing parallels between fishing and talent scouting. In both realms, success depends on preparation, strategy, and patience.

I began to understand that just as there are different types of fish, there are different types of candidates, each with unique qualities and potential. Some are easy to catch, abundant and available. Others require patience, skill, and the perfect conditions to land.

In my role as an HR director, I approached talent scouting with the same meticulous care I had learned from

Coach Scott. I conducted thorough analyses of our operations to identify staffing needs, evaluated peak periods and seasonal demands, and considered the unique culture, values, and customer expectations of our establishment. Much like finding the perfect fishing spot, understanding these elements was crucial in building a high-performance team.

I recalled the precision with which Coach Scott had taught me to cast the line, ensuring it landed in the optimal spot. Similarly, in talent scouting, I identified the right places to look for candidates. This involved partnering with hospitality schools, attending job fairs, and leveraging online platforms to reach a diverse pool of potential hires. I understood that the right bait (a compelling job description, competitive compensation, and a positive company culture) was essential in attracting top talent.

Patience, too, played a significant role. Just as I had waited for the fish to bite, I learned to be patient in the hiring process. Rushing to fill a position often led to poor fit and high turnover. Instead, I focused on thorough screening and assessments, ensuring that each candidate was not only qualified but also aligned with our company's values and goals.

One hiring experience stands out as a testament to these lessons. We were looking for a new front desk manager, a critical role that requires a blend of technical skills and exceptional customer service abilities. I remembered Coach Scott's advice about having as many hooks in the sea as possible. We cast a wide net, reaching out to candidates from various backgrounds and industries.

After several rounds of interviews, we found a candidate who seemed perfect on paper but lacked the spark we were looking for. It was tempting to hire quickly, but I remembered the importance of patience and strategy. We continued our search, and soon, we discovered a candidate who not only had the necessary skills but also exuded warmth and enthusiasm. She had a natural talent for making guests feel welcome and valued, much like the thrill of reeling in a big catch.

The decision to hire her proved to be one of the best we ever made. She brought a fresh perspective to the team, implemented innovative ideas, and significantly improved guest satisfaction scores. It was a reminder that the principles of fishing (preparation, strategy, patience, and using the right bait) were indeed applicable to talent scouting.

Identifying Potential Talent: Lessons from a Diverse Team

In our community of Udhailiyah, soccer was more than just a collection of players; it was a melting pot of cultures, backgrounds, and perspectives. We were a group of American kids playing in a league dominated by British and Canadian teams. Our team, under the guidance of Coach Scott, embodied the principles of diversity and inclusion long before these terms became popular buzzwords.

As we integrated new players, Coach Scott made a conscious effort to eliminate bias in team selection. He focused on skills, potential, and the unique qualities each player could bring to the team. Our practice sessions became a mix of different playing styles, languages, and cultures, creating a dynamic and innovative environment.

To ensure fairness, Coach Scott involved senior players in the selection process. This diverse panel, comprising players from different backgrounds, ensured that selections were made based on merit and the ability to contribute to the team's success. This approach not only built trust but also encouraged us to embrace each other's differences.

Coach Scott understood that while cultural fit was important, a cultural add could be equally valuable. He believed that it was essential for new players to align with the team's core values of teamwork, discipline, and respect, but he also recognized the power of bringing in fresh perspectives that could enhance and evolve our team culture.

One memorable practice highlighted this perfectly. Hatish, a new player who had recently joined us, introduced some training techniques he had learned in Jordan. These drills were unlike anything we had experienced before, emphasizing agility and quick thinking. At first, many of us were skeptical, uncertain about how these new methods would fit into our established routines.

However, as we practiced, it became clear that these techniques brought immense value. They made us faster, more responsive, and ultimately more cohesive as a unit. Coach Scott didn't just watch how players performed during these drills; he observed how they interacted with the team, handled pressure, and contributed to the overall dynamics both on and off the field.

He believed that you could truly gauge someone's talent not just by how they performed within the confines of structured drills but by how they acted outside of the box: how they adapted, how they innovated, and how they inspired others.

Hatish quickly became known not just for his skills but for his supportive nature and willingness to help others improve. His approach aligned perfectly with our team values, yet he brought something new that elevated our performance and strengthened our bond as a team.

Coach Scott's approach to balancing cultural fit with cultural add taught us that true strength comes not just from uniformity but from the diversity of thought and experience that challenges and enhances the team's collective ability.

In essence, a strategic, well-rounded approach to talent scouting is essential for building a high performing hospitality team. The lessons learned from the fishing trip with Coach (patience, strategy, and understanding the environment) apply directly to identifying and attracting top talent. By understanding the difference between active and passive candidates, using behavioral indicators and assessment tools, and looking for talent in educational institutions, other industries, and within your current team, you can build a diverse and culturally aligned workforce.

Recognizing the importance of role specific behaviors, soft skills, and personality traits ensures that new hires meet the expectations of their roles and contribute to the overall success of the organization.

The Art of Giving Feedback

Finding the right talent is only the beginning. Once they're on your team, the real work begins developing that talent, shaping performance, and helping each person reach their full potential. This is where feedback becomes essential.

Yet feedback remains one of the most misunderstood and underutilized tools in hospitality leadership. Too often, feedback is delivered as criticism, saved for annual reviews, or avoided altogether because managers fear uncomfortable conversations. But when done right, feedback is the fuel that drives growth, builds confidence, and creates a culture of continuous improvement.

Bringing It in as a Team: The Feedback Play

The Feedback Play in *The Hospitality Playbook* is about transforming feedback from something people dread into something they seek out. It's about creating an environment where growth is celebrated, mistakes are seen as learning opportunities, and every team member knows exactly where they stand and how to improve.

The Core Principles of Effective Feedback

Be Specific and Timely

Vague feedback is useless feedback. "Good job" tells someone nothing. "Great job managing that difficult guest situation by staying calm, listening to their concerns, and finding a creative solution that left them satisfied" gives someone a roadmap of exactly what to repeat.

Similarly, feedback delayed is feedback diminished. The moment something happens (good or bad) is when the learning opportunity is strongest. Waiting weeks or months for a formal review means the context is lost, the emotions have faded, and the opportunity to adjust behavior has passed.

In hospitality, where every interaction matters and the pace is relentless, timely feedback becomes even more critical. A server who receives immediate feedback on how they handled a rush can apply that learning to the next shift. Wait two weeks, and the lesson loses its power.

Focus on Behavior, Not Character

There's a profound difference between "You're disorganized" and "I noticed the reservation system wasn't updated after your shift, which caused confusion for the morning team." The first attacks someone's identity. The second identifies a specific behavior that can be changed.

Coach Scott taught me this distinction early. After a game where I'd let in a goal, he didn't say "You're a bad goalkeeper." He said, "You're positioning on that corner kick left the near post exposed. Let's work on your angles." Same information, completely different impact. One made me want to quit. The other made me want to get better.

When giving feedback, describe what you observed, explain the impact, and discuss how to improve. Keep it about actions, not essence.

Balance Positive and Constructive

Feedback that's exclusively critical demoralizes. Feedback that's exclusively positive creates complacency. The sweet spot is balance: recognizing what's working while identifying opportunities for growth.

This doesn't mean the artificial "feedback sandwich" where you say something nice, deliver criticism, then say something nice again. People see through that instantly. Instead, it means genuinely looking for both strengths and areas for development and addressing both with equal honesty and care.

When I see a team member excel at something, I tell them specifically what they did well and why it mattered. When I see an opportunity for improvement, I frame it as growth: "Here's what you're already doing well. Here's where I think you could be even more effective."

Make It a Dialogue, not a Monologue

Feedback shouldn't be a one-way lecture. The most powerful feedback happens in conversation, where both people are actively engaged in problem solving.

Ask questions. "What do you think went well?" "Where do you think you could improve?" "What support do you need from me?" When people identify their own areas for growth, they're far more invested in making changes. I learned this from Coach Scott during our fishing trip.

He didn't just tell me what I was doing wrong with my casting technique. He asked me what I noticed, what I felt, what I thought might work better. By drawing out my own observations, he made me an active participant in my improvement rather than a passive recipient of criticism.

Connect Feedback to Goals

Every piece of feedback should be connected to something larger: the person's professional development, the team's objectives, or the organization's mission. When people understand why feedback matters, they're more likely to act on it.

"I'm giving you this feedback because I see leadership potential in you, and this skill will be critical as you advance." That statement transforms feedback from criticism into investment. It shows you're not just correcting mistakes; you're developing talent.

Creating a Feedback Rich Culture

Individual feedback conversations matter, but the real transformation happens when you create a culture where feedback flows naturally in all directions: manager to employee, employee to manager, peer to peer.

Normalize Ongoing Feedback

Instead of saving all feedback for formal reviews, integrate it into daily operations. After a shift, take five minutes to highlight what went well and discuss one thing to improve next time. After a challenging guest interaction, debrief immediately while the experience is fresh.

Make feedback so routine that it becomes unremarkable. When feedback is constant and mostly positive, the occasional constructive feedback doesn't feel like an attack; it feels like helpful guidance.

Model Receptiveness

If you want your team to be open to feedback, you must model that openness yourself. Ask your team for feedback on your leadership. "What could I do differently to support you better?" "What's one thing I should stop doing?" "How can I improve our team meetings?"

When you receive feedback, listen without defensiveness. Thank the person for their honesty. If appropriate, act on what you hear. When your team sees you accepting and implementing feedback, they'll be far more willing to do the same.

Celebrating Growth

When someone implements feedback and improves, acknowledge it publicly. "I want to recognize Sarah for the work she's put into her time management. Three weeks ago, we talked about strategies for staying organized during busy shifts, and I've seen real improvement. Great job."

This serves multiple purposes: it reinforces positive behavior, shows that you notice improvement, and demonstrates to the entire team that feedback leads to growth and recognition.

The Coaching Mindset

Hospitality leaders are encouraged to adopt a coaching mindset when giving feedback, much like Coach Scott did on the fishing trip. This approach means viewing feedback as a tool for guiding team members toward their full potential.

Rather than waiting for formal review periods, managers should integrate feedback into daily interactions, providing real time insights and celebrating incremental improvements. This ongoing feedback loop reinforces a culture of excellence and keeps employees engaged, motivated, and aligned with the organization's goals. A coaching mindset asks: "How can I help this person get better?" rather than "How can I point out what they're doing wrong?" It's fundamentally about development rather than judgment.

Personal Reflection: Lessons from the Fishing Trip and Talent Scouting

Reflecting on my journey from the soccer field to hospitality, I see how Coach Scott's approach to feedback has influenced my leadership style. His lessons, particularly those taught during our fishing trip, emphasized patience, specificity, and the value of ongoing guidance.

Just as he helped me improve my casting technique one step at a time, I strive to guide my team members with clear, actionable feedback that fosters growth without diminishing confidence.

One experience in particular stands out. During my time as an HR director, I worked with a team member who was exceptionally dedicated but struggled with time management. Rather than addressing it as a flaw, I approached the feedback the way Coach Scott would: by identifying specific behaviors and suggesting practical solutions.

Together, we developed a plan that included small, manageable goals. We broke down his shifts into segments, created checklists for closing procedures, and set up a simple system for prioritizing tasks during rushes. We met weekly to discuss what was working and what needed adjustment.

This approach helped him improve his time management skills without feeling overwhelmed. Over time, he became more efficient and confident, and his contributions to the team grew significantly. More importantly, he began asking for feedback proactively, seeing it as a resource rather than a threat.

That transformation reminded me of Coach Scott's lesson on the jetty: growth happens one cast at a time, with patience, guidance, and the willingness to keep trying.

Implementing The Feedback Play: Practical Steps

For hospitality leaders, implementing the Feedback Play involves fostering an environment where growth and learning are celebrated. Here are some practical steps:

Schedule Regular Check Ins: Make feedback a routine part of the work environment by scheduling regular one on one meetings with team members to discuss their progress and address any concerns. These don't need to be lengthy; even 15-minute check ins can be powerful if they're consistent and focused.

Use Clear, Actionable Language: Ensure that feedback focuses on specific, observable behaviors, and offer practical suggestions for improvement rather than vague critiques. Instead of "Be more professional," try "When guests approach the desk, make eye contact, smile, and greet them within five seconds. This creates an immediate positive impression."

Balance Positive and Constructive Feedback: Recognize achievements and strengths while providing constructive guidance on areas for growth. A balanced approach helps build confidence and fosters resilience. Remember that your job is to help people become their best selves, not to create perfect robots who never make mistakes.

Encourage Open Dialogue: Make feedback a two-way conversation by inviting team members to share their thoughts, ask questions, and contribute to their development. Questions like "What do you think?" and "How do you see this situation?" transform monologues into collaborations.

Celebrating Incremental Progress: Acknowledge small improvements and celebrate milestones. This reinforces the idea that growth is a journey and that every step forward is an achievement. The server who reduced their average table turn time by two minutes deserves recognition just as much as the manager who exceeded revenue targets.

Document Progress: Keep notes on feedback conversations and the progress you observe. This serves multiple purposes: it shows you're paying attention, it provides data for formal reviews, and it helps you track patterns over time. When you can say "Three months ago we talked about X, and I've seen consistent improvement," that's powerful validation.

Create Peer Feedback Opportunities: Encourage team members to give each other constructive feedback. This might involve structured peer reviews, mentorship pairings, or simply creating a culture where teammates help each other improve. When feedback comes from multiple sources, it's more credible and less threatening.

Link Feedback to Development Plans: Connect feedback to each person's career aspirations. "I'm giving you this feedback because developing this skill is essential for the leadership role you're working toward." This transforms feedback from correction into career development.

The Feedback Commitment

By embracing these practices, hospitality leaders can create a culture where feedback is not just a tool for correction but a catalyst for personal and professional growth. The Feedback Play becomes more than a managerial tactic; it becomes an investment in each team member's potential, building a team that is engaged, motivated, and dedicated to excellence.

Feedback, when done well, is an act of respect. It says: "I see you. I believe in you. I'm invested in your growth." It acknowledges that everyone has room to improve and that improvement is possible, expected, and supported.

Just as Coach Scott stood beside me on that jetty in Half Moon Bay, patiently teaching me to cast my line with precision, hospitality leaders must stand beside their teams, offering guidance, encouragement, and honest feedback that help each person become better at their craft.

The fish didn't catch themselves that day. I needed Coach Scott's wisdom, patience, and specific guidance to land the big one. Your team is no different. They need your feedback to reach their potential.

Give it generously. Give it specifically. Give it with care.

Because when feedback flows freely and constructively, teams don't just perform better. They grow together, trust each other, and become capable of achievements none of them could have achieved alone.

That's the power of the Feedback Play. That's what transforms good teams into great ones. That's what separates organizations that retain talent from those that constantly recruit to replace it.

Cast your line. Be patient. Use the right bait. And help your team reel in their best selves.

Play #4 The Career Play

The Tryout & The Setup

It was the start of a new soccer season, and Coach Scott had just wrapped up a grueling practice session. We were all exhausted, dripping with sweat, and gasping for breath. The Saudi sun had been relentless, and every muscle in my body screamed for rest.

But Coach Scott had other plans.

He called me over, his expression serious yet encouraging.

"We need new players, and I want you to help me with the tryouts," he said. "Think of this as an interview process. We're not just looking for the best players; we're looking for the right players for our team."

Coach Scott's words resonated with me. Preparation was crucial. Just like preparing for a business interview, we needed to understand what we were looking for in the new players. We spent the next few days going over the team's needs, the positions we needed to fill, and the qualities that would make a good fit for our team.

"We need a strong defender, someone who can hold the line and not get rattled under pressure," Coach Scott explained. "We also need a midfielder with excellent vision, someone who can control the game and create opportunities."

I realized that understanding the specific needs of the team was akin to understanding the requirements of a job position. It was essential to have a clear picture of what we were looking for before we began the tryouts. We weren't just filling positions; we were building a team that could work together, complement each other's strengths, and cover each other's weaknesses.

Building Rapport

The day of the tryouts arrived. Young hopefuls from various backgrounds gathered on the field, each one eager to prove their worth. The nervous energy was palpable. Some kids bounced on their toes. Others stretched obsessively. A few stood perfectly still, eyes fixed on Coach Scott.

Coach Scott emphasized the importance of building rapport with the candidates.

"Start with small talk," he advised. "Make them feel comfortable. When they're relaxed, they'll perform better, and you'll get a more accurate read on their abilities." I approached the first candidate, a tall, lanky boy with nervous energy radiating off him like heat.

"Hey there," I said, smiling. "What's your name? Where are you from?" As we chatted, I could see him relax. His shoulders loosened, and he began to speak more freely about his love for soccer, his previous teams, his favorite position. Building rapport was not just about putting the candidates at ease; it was about creating a connection and understanding their motivations. Why were they here? What drove them? What did soccer mean to them?

Structured and Unstructured Assessment

Coach Scott believed in a balanced approach to evaluation.

"We need a mix of structured and unstructured questions," he explained. "Structured questions ensure consistency, but unstructured observation can reveal deeper insights."

We began with structured drills, assessing each player's technical skills. We had them run through a series of exercises, from dribbling to passing to shooting. This was the structured part of the tryout, where we could objectively measure their abilities. Who could control the ball under pressure? Who had accuracy in their passes? Who could finish when it counted?

But it was during the unstructured part of the tryout that we learned the most about the candidates.

We set up a scrimmage match, allowing the players to interact naturally. It was here that we observed their decision making, teamwork, and how they handled pressure. The clipboard got put down. The stopwatch got ignored. This was about watching how people played when no one was grading them.

One player stood out during the scrimmage. He wasn't the fastest or the strongest, but his vision and understanding of the game were exceptional. He directed his teammates, created opportunities, and maintained his composure under pressure. When someone made a mistake, he encouraged them. When the team needed direction, he provided it. It was clear that he had the qualities we were looking for in a midfielder.

Understanding Past Behavior

Coach Scott introduced me to the concept of behavioral interview questions.

"Past behavior is the best predictor of future performance," he said. "Ask them about specific situations and how they handled them." We gathered the candidates after the scrimmage and began a series of one-on-one interviews. I asked the standout midfielder, "Can you describe a time when you had to lead your team through a challenging match?"

He recounted a story of a high stakes game where his team was down by two goals at halftime. Instead of panicking, he rallied his teammates in the locker room, helped them refocus their strategy, and led them to a comeback draw in the final minutes. His response demonstrated leadership, resilience, and strategic thinking: qualities that aligned perfectly with our team's needs.

Practical Tests Under Pressure

Coach Scott believed in the power of practical tests and role-playing scenarios.

"You can learn a lot about a player's character by putting them in real life situations," he said.

We set up various scenarios on the field, from defending a lead in the final minutes to breaking through a tight defense. Each candidate had the opportunity to showcase their skills and decision making in these high-pressure situations. These weren't the clean, controlled drills from earlier. These were messy, chaotic, real.

One candidate, a defender, excelled during these tests. In a scenario where he had to defend a narrow lead with only minutes remaining, he organized the backline, communicated effectively with his teammates, and made crucial interceptions. His ability to stay calm and focused under pressure was impressive. While others panicked or got frustrated, he got clearer and more decisive.

Reading Non-Verbal Cues

Coach Scott had an uncanny ability to read people, and he taught me to pay attention to non-verbal cues.

"Body language, eye contact, and how they carry themselves can tell you a lot about a person," he said. During the interviews and practical tests, I observed the candidates closely. The midfielder who had stood out earlier maintained eye contact, had a confident posture, and exuded quiet authority. When he spoke, people listened. When he moved, people followed.

In contrast, another candidate who performed well technically seemed shifty and avoided eye contact, raising concerns about his confidence and reliability. His skills were solid, but something felt off. Coach Scott noticed it too.

"Technical skills you can teach," Coach Scott said quietly. "Character is harder to change."

Envisioning Fit and Future Potential

The tryouts were not just about assessing current skills but also about envisioning each candidate's fit and potential within the team. Coach Scott emphasized the importance of looking beyond immediate abilities.

"Think about how they will grow with the team," he said. "Do they have the potential to take on more responsibilities? Can they adapt and improve?

"I pondered this as we reviewed the candidates. The standout midfielder showed great potential for growth. His leadership qualities and understanding of the game suggested that he could become a key player in the future. The defender, with his calm demeanor and strong organizational skills, also showed promise for a leadership role.

Coach Scott believed in identifying candidates with leadership potential.

"We need players who can step up and lead when needed," he said. "Look for traits like initiative, decision making ability, and a willingness to take on additional responsibilities."

We asked the candidates about their aspirations and how they saw themselves growing within the team. The standout midfielder expressed a desire to mentor younger players and eventually take on a coaching role. His ambition and vision aligned with our long-term goals for the team.

Lessons Learned

As the tryouts concluded, I reflected on the lessons I had learned from Coach Scott. Conducting effective interviews was about more than just assessing technical skills. It required a holistic approach, considering behavioral traits, potential for growth, and overall fit within the team.

The structured recruitment process we had followed (from preparation and building rapport to structured and unstructured evaluation, practical tests, and envisioning fit and potential) had provided a comprehensive understanding of each candidate. The standout midfielder and the calm defender were selected to join our team. Their inclusion not only strengthened our squad but also brought in qualities that would contribute to the team's long-term success.

Reflecting on this experience, I realized that the principles of effective interviewing applied not only to soccer but also to the hospitality industry. Understanding the specific needs of the team, preparing thoroughly, building rapport, and assessing both technical skills and behavioral traits were crucial in finding the right candidates.

Coach Scott's lessons have stayed with me throughout my career, shaping my approach to recruitment and leadership. The structured recruitment process, inspired by soccer tryouts, has become a cornerstone of my professional success, helping me build high performing teams that align with our vision and values.

People Watching

One of the most insightful lessons I learned about interviewing came not from an office but from the bleachers of a soccer field. Sitting with Coach Scott, we watched another team play. Observing how the players acted before, during, and after the game provided a wealth of information about their behaviors, attitudes, and teamwork.

Some players displayed leadership. Others panicked under pressure. A few showcased remarkable resilience. Coach Scott had a way of describing players that made patterns instantly recognizable. "See that one?" he'd say, pointing to a player who dominated the field with confidence and strength. "That's your lion. Natural leader, commands respect, takes charge in critical moments."

Then he'd nod toward another player, quick and calculating. "And that one's a fox. Strategic, always thinking three moves ahead, finds creative solutions." This exercise in people watching translated directly into understanding candidates during interviews. Observing how candidates react to questions, their body language, and their interactions can reveal much about their potential fit and performance. Are they confident or defensive? Do they listen before responding? How do they handle disagreement or challenges? The best insights often come not from what people say but from how they say it and what they do when they think no one is watching.

Building a Winning Team

The Underdogs: A Journey to the Playoffs

It was my final year in Saudi Arabia, and our soccer team was a mix of seasoned players and new faces. We had ended the regular season as a wildcard team, barely making it into the playoffs. The memory of our defeats at the hands of the Cougars, our fiercest rivals, still stung. They were the team that had laughed at me during my first practice, a team that seemed unbeatable.

Coach Scott, with his wisdom and unyielding belief in our potential, gathered us for a pep talk.

"We may be the underdogs, but we have something they don't: heart and unity," he said. "Winning isn't just about talent; it's about working together and believing in each other."

His words resonated deeply with us. We knew that if we were to stand any chance, we needed to function as a cohesive unit. Each player had to understand their role and how it contributed to the team's success.

Our first playoff match was against a strong team known for their aggressive play. Coach Scott emphasized the importance of discipline and strategy.

"Stick to the plan, support each other, and stay focused," he urged.

We played with determination, each player giving their all. Our defense held strong, our midfield controlled the game, and our forwards took every opportunity. The match ended in our favor, a hard-fought victory that boosted our confidence.

With each subsequent match, our teamwork improved. We communicated better, anticipated each other's moves, and covered one another's weaknesses. Coach Scott's training sessions, which focused on both technical skills and team dynamics, paid off. We won our way through the playoffs, defying the odds and building momentum that carried us to the championship match against the Cougars.

The championship game was everything we had worked toward. Facing the Cougars again, the team that had dominated us all season, we knew this was our chance to prove ourselves. The match was intense, every moment charged with tension and determination.

In the final minutes, with the score tied, I faced a penalty kick that could determine the outcome. My heart pounded as I stepped up to the ball. I remembered Coach Scott's words, the countless hours of practice, and the faith my teammates had in me. I took a deep breath, focused, and kicked.

The ball sailed past the goalkeeper and into the net.

We won. We were champions.

The celebration that followed was unforgettable, but more than the trophy, it was the journey we had taken together that mattered most. We had grown as individuals and as a team, learning the value of perseverance, unity, and belief in each other.

Bringing It in as a Team: The Career Path Play

In sports, the most successful teams are those that invest in their players' development, nurturing their skills and preparing them for greater responsibilities. Similarly, the Career Path Play in hospitality focuses on creating clear, meaningful career trajectories that give employees a reason to stay and grow within the organization.

The Career Path Play is about showing employees that they're not just filling a position; they're building a career. It's about demonstrating that the organization values their growth and has a vision for their future. When employees can see a path forward, they invest more deeply in their work and remain committed to the organization.

The Core Elements of Career Development

Create Clear Career Pathways

Just as a soccer player progresses from junior leagues to varsity to potentially professional levels, hospitality employees need to see clear pathways for advancement. This means defining what skills, experiences, and competencies are required for each level within the organization.

In my career, I've seen too many talented employees leave because they couldn't envision their future. They looked around and saw the same job they were doing, just five years from now, maybe with a slightly better title. That's not inspiring. That's depressing.

Clear career pathways change that equation. When a front desk agent can see that developing certain skills will lead to a supervisor role, and that supervisor role can lead to management, and that management experience can lead to director level positions, suddenly they have something to work toward. They have a reason to invest in their own development.

Provide Training and Development Opportunities

Career paths without training are just wishful thinking. Organizations must invest in developing their employees' skills through formal training programs, mentorship opportunities, and hands on learning experiences.

Coach Scott didn't just tell us we could be better players; he trained us relentlessly. He worked with us individually on our weaknesses, celebrated our strengths, and pushed us to expand our capabilities. The same principle applies in hospitality.

Training should be tailored in both technical and interpersonal skills. A server who wants to become a manager needs customer service excellence, but they also need to learn leadership, conflict resolution, financial management, and strategic thinking. Provide the training that bridges the gap between where they are and where they want to be.

Offering Mentorship Programs

Mentorship accelerates development in ways that formal training alone cannot. When experienced leaders take newer employees under their wing, knowledge transfer happens organically, relationships deepen, and cultural values get passed down naturally.

I learned more from Coach Scott through our conversations, our fishing trips, and watching how he handled challenges than I ever could have learned from a textbook. The same holds true in hospitality. A mentor can provide real world wisdom, help navigate organizational politics, offer career advice, and serve as a sounding board for ideas and challenges. Effective mentorship programs pair employees with mentors who can guide their development, provide feedback, and help them navigate their career path. This creates a culture of growth and investment that benefits both the mentor and the mentee.

Recognize and Reward Progress

As employees develop their skills and take on new responsibilities, recognition and reward are essential. This might include promotions, increased compensation, expanded responsibilities, or public acknowledgment of their growth. When we won games in soccer, Coach Scott celebrated our victories. When individual players showed improvement, he recognized it publicly. This recognition motivated us to keep pushing, keep improving, keep striving for excellence.

In hospitality, recognizing career progress reinforces the message that growth is valued and rewarded. It motivates other employees to pursue their own development and creates a culture where advancement is both possible and celebrated.

Support Lateral Movement

Not all career growth is vertical. Sometimes the best development comes from lateral moves that broaden an employee's skill set and deepen their understanding of the organization.

A front desk supervisor who moves into event planning gains new skills and perspectives. A restaurant manager who spends time in catering learns a different side of the business. These lateral moves create more versatile, well-rounded employees who understand how different parts of the organization interconnect.

In soccer, Coach Scott sometimes moved players to different positions to help them develop new skills and better understand the game from different perspectives. The midfielder who spent time playing defense became better at reading defensive formations. The forward who played midfield learned to create opportunities rather than just finish them.

In hospitality, lateral growth opportunities can have a similar impact. By allowing employees to move into different departments or roles that better align with their strengths or interests, organizations can retain talent that might otherwise seek opportunities elsewhere. Employees gain diverse experiences, which not only boosts their skills but also gives them a deeper understanding of the company, making them more invested and engaged in their work.

Strategy: The Career Path Play in Action

The Career Path Play requires a proactive approach, where managers don't wait for employees to seek growth but actively guide them through their potential career trajectories. This play reduces turnover by showing employees that the organization values their development and has a long-term vision for their careers. When employees feel they are working toward something greater, they are more likely to stay loyal and committed.

Identify Employee Strengths and Goals

Hold career discussions with each team member to understand their skills, aspirations, and areas for growth. Just as a coach learns about each player's potential, managers should invest time in learning about their team members' career goals.

These conversations should happen regularly, not just during annual reviews. Ask questions: Where do you see yourself in two years? Five years? What skills do you want to develop? What roles interest you? What would make you excited to come to work every day?

Listen carefully to the answers. Not everyone wants to climb the traditional career ladder. Some people want to become the absolute best in their current role. Others want to move laterally to explore different areas. Some dream of management. Others prefer to be individual contributors with deep expertise. Understanding what each person wants allows you to tailor development plans that motivate them.

Develop Training Programs

Create a mix of formal training sessions, hands on learning, and mentorship opportunities. Tailor training to both the technical and interpersonal skills required in hospitality, ensuring that employees feel equipped to excel and grow.

Training should be accessible, relevant, and tied directly to career advancement. When an employee knows that completing a specific training program will qualify them for promotion consideration, that training becomes meaningful rather than just another box to check.

Consider creating a leadership development program for high potential employees. Include topics like financial management, conflict resolution, performance management, strategic planning, and emotional intelligence. Give participants real projects to work on that benefit the organization while developing their skills.

Define Advancement Criteria

Clearly communicate the expectations and criteria for career advancement within the organization. This transparency empowers employees to work toward their goals with a clear understanding of what's required to move forward.

Ambiguity kills motivation. When employees don't know what it takes to get promoted, they either assume it's political (who you know) or arbitrary (luck). Neither assumption inspires effort or loyalty.

Instead, be crystal clear: "To be considered for a supervisor role, you need to demonstrate proficiency in these five areas, complete this training, and successfully lead a project team. Here's how we'll measure your readiness."

Transparency removes mystery and replaces it with a roadmap. Employees can then take ownership of their own advancement by deliberately working on the areas that need development.

Offer Lateral Opportunities

Encourage employees to explore different roles within the organization by offering lateral moves. This approach builds versatility and strengthens the organization by creating a workforce with diverse experiences and perspectives.

Make lateral movement easy and encouraged rather than difficult and stigmatized. Too often, lateral moves are seen as failures or steps backward. Reframe them as strategic development opportunities that create more well-rounded professionals.

A food and beverage manager who moves into rooms division learns the hotel business more comprehensively.

When they eventually move into a general manager role, that diverse background makes them more effective. The investment in lateral development pays dividends throughout their career.

Celebrate and Acknowledge Growth

Recognize milestones in employees' career paths, whether it's completing a training program, taking on a new role, or achieving a promotion. Celebrating growth reinforces the organization's commitment to development and motivates employees to continue pursuing their career goals.

Make career development victories as visible as operational successes. When someone completes a significant training program, announce it. When someone takes on a new role, celebrate their progression. When someone gets promoted, share their story and the path they took to get there.

These celebrations serve multiple purposes: they recognize individual achievement, they demonstrate that career development is valued, and they show other employees that advancement is possible and happening.

Personal Reflection: From Tryouts to Career Paths

Looking back, the tryout process with Coach Scott taught me invaluable lessons about talent development and long-term growth. Through the structured yet flexible process he used, I saw firsthand the impact of clear expectations, tailored guidance, and the importance of considering both immediate needs and future potential. These lessons have stayed with me throughout my career in hospitality, where I've learned that the best teams are those built not only for today's needs but also with an eye toward the future.

One experience stands out from my time as an HR director in hospitality. We were searching for a new front desk manager, a role that required both technical skills and a warm, customer-oriented demeanor. While one candidate met all the technical requirements perfectly, another candidate, though slightly less experienced, showed exceptional people skills and a natural talent for making guests feel welcome.

I watched her during the interview process. She remembered names. She asked thoughtful questions. She showed genuine curiosity about the role and the organization. Most tellingly, she treated everyone she encountered (from the receptionist to the general manager) with the same respect and warmth.

Remembering Coach Scott's approach to evaluating potential over perfection, I advocated for the latter candidate, understanding that with the right training and support, she could grow into the role beautifully. There was initial resistance. Why take a chance on someone less experienced when we have a perfectly qualified candidate?

But I had learned from Coach Scott that you don't just hire for today; you hire for tomorrow and next year and five years from now. You hire people with the capacity and desire to grow.

We hired her. We invested in her training. We provided mentorship and support.

Over time, she became not just competent but exceptional. She developed the technical skills quickly, but her natural warmth and genuine care for guests set her apart. She eventually became one of our most valued leaders, and the decision to invest in her growth proved invaluable to the entire organization.

That experience reinforced what Coach Scott had taught me: look for potential, invest in development, and give people the opportunity to grow into roles rather than only hiring people who are already perfect fits. The latter approach fills positions. The former builds teams.

Building a Future Together

The Career Path Play is ultimately about building a future together with employees. When leaders invest in their team members' growth, they create a culture of loyalty and mutual success. Much like a coach who nurtures a player's development over seasons, hospitality leaders can guide employees on their career journeys, helping them achieve both personal and organizational goals.

By implementing this play, organizations send a powerful message: this isn't just a place for a job; it's a place for a career. This approach fosters a sense of purpose and belonging, making employees feel valued and understood.

When someone can look at their organization and see not just where they are but where they can be, something shifts. They stop thinking short term (what's my next paycheck?) and start thinking long term (what's my future here?). That shift transforms the employment relationship from transactional to meaningful.

Employees who see a future invest differently. They take initiative. They seek feedback. They volunteer for challenging assignments. They mentor others. They bring ideas for improvement. They think like owners rather than renters.

This transformation doesn't happen by accident. It happens when organizations deliberately create the structures, programs, and culture that support career development. It happens when leaders make career conversations a priority. It happens when training budgets are protected even in tough times. It happens when promotions come from within rather than always hiring externally.

As hospitality leaders build their teams, they're not just creating a staff; they're building a community of professionals who are committed, skilled, and ready to grow with the organization.

The Career Path Play transforms the workplace from a steppingstone into a destination, where employees can envision a meaningful, long-term career. Just as athletes train season after season to reach new heights, hospitality employees will feel motivated and inspired by a clear vision of where they're headed.

This play isn't just about individual advancement; it's about building a winning team and a thriving culture that attracts, retains, and develops top talent for the long haul.

When you walked into our final championship game as underdogs and walked out as champions, it wasn't because we had the most talented individual players. It was because we had developed each person's potential, created clear roles, invested in our growth, and believed in what we could accomplish together.

That's what the Career Path Play creates in hospitality: teams that exceed expectations not because they started with the most talent, but because they developed it, nurtured it, and gave it room to flourish.

Invest in your people's futures, and they'll invest in yours. Show them a path, and they'll walk it with you. Build their careers, and they'll build your organization.

That's the promise and power of the Career Path Play.

Lessons from the Field: The Seeds of Learning

My journey has been one of growth, shaped by lessons learned from two influential coaches and the countless adventures of my travels. Coach Scott and Coach Reynolds were more than just mentors on the soccer field; they were life teachers who imparted wisdom that has guided me through various challenges and successes.

Coach Scott: Discipline and Resilience

In Saudi Arabia, Coach Scott was my first real mentor. He taught me the fundamentals of soccer, but more importantly, he taught me about discipline, resilience, and the importance of teamwork. Coach Scott ran a tight ship. Practices were structured and intense, with a clear focus on developing both our physical skills and mental toughness. He believed that discipline on the field translated to discipline in life.

One scorching afternoon, during a particularly grueling practice, I remember wanting to give up. The sun beat down mercilessly. My legs felt like lead, and my lungs were on fire. Every breath felt like inhaling razors. Sweat poured into my eyes, stinging and blurring my vision.

Sensing my struggle, Coach Scott pulled me aside.

"Success isn't about how you start; it's about how you finish," he said, his hand on my shoulder. "Push through the pain, stay focused, and you'll come out stronger."

His words stuck with me. They taught me that discipline and perseverance are crucial, not just in sports, but in all aspects of life. Whether it's a challenging project at work or a personal goal, staying disciplined and seeing things through to the end is essential.

Our team was often the underdog in many matches. The Cougars, our fiercest rivals, had a reputation for being unbeatable. We faced them numerous times and often came up short. But Coach Scott never let us dwell on our losses. Instead, he used them as learning opportunities.

"Every setback is a setup for a comeback," he would say.

After each defeat, we would analyze our performance, identify areas for improvement, and work even harder. This resilience paid off when we finally defeated the Cougars in a dramatic championship match. The victory was sweet, not just because we won, but because of the journey we had taken to get there.

This lesson in resilience has been invaluable. Life is filled with setbacks, but it's our response to them that defines us. Embracing challenges, learning from failures, and persistently striving for improvement are key to personal and professional growth.

Travel: Adaptability and Cultural Awareness

My travels between Saudi Arabia and the United States were filled with adventures that further enriched my understanding of the world and my place in it. Traveling alone as a teenager, I had to adapt quickly to different environments. Navigating airports, dealing with delays, and finding my way in unfamiliar cities taught me to stay calm and think on my feet.

One memorable trip involved a layover in Paris. I had missed my connecting flight and had to navigate the complexities of rebooking. Despite the language barrier and initial frustration, I managed to get on the next flight. The airport was massive and confusing. The announcements were all in French. The ticket agents spoke minimal English. I was exhausted, frustrated, and more than a little scared.

But I took a breath, found someone who could help, used gestures and my limited French, and eventually worked it out. This experience taught me the importance of staying flexible and resourceful, skills that have been invaluable in both my personal and professional life. When things don't go according to plan (and they rarely do), you adapt. You figure it out. You keep moving forward.

Living in Saudi Arabia and traveling to various countries exposed me to diverse cultures and perspectives. This exposure cultivated a deep sense of empathy and cultural awareness.

I remember a trip to a local market in Saudi Arabia with my family. The vibrant colors, the rich aromas, and the bustling energy were mesmerizing. Spices piled in pyramids of crimson, gold, and deep brown. The smell of cardamom and saffron mixing with grilled meat and fresh bread. Vendors calling out their wares in Arabic, gesturing enthusiastically. The press of bodies, the heat, the life.

Engaging with the local vendors and learning about their traditions broadened my horizons and deepened my appreciation for cultural diversity. In the hospitality industry, understanding and respecting cultural differences is crucial. This awareness helps in providing personalized and respectful service to guests from all over the world.

Coach Reynolds: Unity and Leadership

Returning to the States, I encountered Coach Reynolds, whose teachings further honed my skills and understanding of leadership and teamwork. Coach Reynolds believed in the strength of the collective.

"A team is more than just a group of individuals; it's a family," he would say.

He emphasized the importance of trust, communication, and mutual support. During a summer camp, Coach Reynolds organized numerous team building activities. One particularly memorable exercise involved a trust fall, where each team member had to fall backward, trusting their teammates to catch them.

The exercise was nerve wracking but incredibly bonding. Standing at the edge, preparing to fall, your entire body resists. Every instinct scream to protect yourself. But you must override that instinct and trust. Trust that your teammates will be there. Trust that they'll catch you. Trust that they care enough to keep you safe.

It taught us to rely on each other and to understand that our success depended on our ability to work together. This lesson in teamwork has been pivotal in my professional life. In the hospitality industry, collaboration and trust among team members are essential for delivering exceptional service. Building a strong, cohesive team can achieve far more than any individual effort.

Coach Reynolds also taught me about the importance of leadership and mentorship. He led by example, always available for advice and support, and encouraged us to mentor younger players.

One day, he asked me to take a new player under my wing. Initially, I was hesitant, feeling that I wasn't experienced enough to be a mentor. But Coach Reynolds assured me, "Leadership isn't about being the best; it's about making others better."

Guiding the new player, I learned the value of patience, communication, and leading by example. This experience showed me that leadership is about empowering others and helping them reach their potential. It's not about your own glory; it's about elevating everyone around you.

The Foundation of Everything

The lessons from Coach Scott, Coach Reynolds, and my travel adventures have profoundly shaped my approach to life and work. Discipline, resilience, teamwork, leadership, adaptability, and cultural awareness are not just abstract concepts but lived experiences that guide my actions and decisions.

Building a winning team, whether on the soccer field or in a professional setting, requires a blend of these qualities. It's about fostering a supportive and inclusive culture, embracing challenges, and continuously striving for improvement. It's about leading by example, mentoring others, and appreciating the rich tapestry of human experiences.

As I continue my journey, I carry these lessons with me, constantly inspired by the wisdom and experiences of my past. They serve as a compass, guiding me toward a future where I can make a positive impact and help others.

Play #5 The Inclusion Play

Bringing It in as a Team: The Inclusion Play

In any team, inclusivity is essential for creating unity and mutual respect among members. Just as a sports coach values every player's contribution regardless of their background, skill level, or experience, leaders in the hospitality industry need to foster a culture where everyone feels valued.

The Inclusion Play focuses on creating an environment where diversity is celebrated, open dialogue is encouraged, and fair practices ensure every employee feels respected. This inclusiveness builds a cohesive team that works together toward shared goals, enhancing both engagement and performance.

But here's the truth: inclusion isn't automatic. It doesn't happen just because you hire diverse candidates or put up a poster about respect. Inclusion requires intentional effort, consistent practice, and genuine commitment from leadership. It's about creating a culture where everyone doesn't just show up; they belong.

Celebrating Diversity

Just as a coach recognizes that each player brings unique skills and perspectives to the team, hospitality leaders should celebrate diversity within their workforce. Embracing diversity allows employees to bring their full selves to work, which enriches the organization with different perspectives, experiences, and ideas.

In the hospitality industry, where employees interact with guests from various cultural backgrounds, a diverse team is invaluable. Employees who feel encouraged to express their unique backgrounds often bring creative solutions and insights that enhance guest experiences.

But celebrating diversity goes beyond hiring people who look different. It means creating an environment where different thinking styles are welcomed, where various approaches to problem solving are valued, where cultural traditions are respected and acknowledged, and where everyone's contributions are seen as essential rather than optional.

Growing up, my experiences with Coach Scott taught me early on about the power of diversity. Our soccer team was made up of players from various backgrounds: American, British, Canadian, and even a few local kids from Saudi Arabia. Coach Scott saw this diversity not as a challenge but as a strength.

He would often say, "A team is only as strong as its range of skills and perspectives."

Each player brought something unique, and Coach encouraged us to learn from each other. The British kids played with a different tactical awareness. The Canadians brought a physical style. The Americans had speed and athleticism. The local Saudi players understood the heat and conditions in ways we never could. This diversity made us more adaptable and helped us approach challenges from multiple angles.

In one memorable match against a tough opponent, our diverse playing styles became our advantage. We were down at halftime, and our usual strategy wasn't working. During the break, Coach Scott asked us what we were seeing, what ideas we had. The British players suggested a tactical shift. The Canadian players offered a more aggressive defensive approach. The American players wanted to use our speed on the counterattack.

Instead of choosing one approach, Coach Scott found a way to incorporate all of them. The adaptability we had developed by embracing each other's strengths and learning different tactics from one another allowed us to pivot our strategy mid game, catching our opponents off guard. We came back to win.

It was a powerful reminder that diversity isn't just about bringing people together; it's about creating a team where every perspective has value. This lesson in embracing diversity stayed with me and has proven invaluable in my hospitality career, where understanding and celebrating cultural differences is essential for building a strong team and delivering exceptional service.

Promoting an Inclusive Culture

An inclusive culture goes beyond mere acknowledgment of diversity; it fosters an environment where every employee feels welcome, valued, and understood. Hospitality managers should take an active role in promoting a sense of belonging among team members, ensuring that employees feel comfortable sharing their ideas, insights, and concerns. This inclusiveness strengthens team cohesion and helps prevent turnover, as employees are more likely to stay with an organization where they feel respected and valued.

When I moved back to the United States, Coach Reynolds became my mentor, emphasizing the importance of unity and support within the team. He believed that each team member should feel like a valued part of the whole. To build this inclusive culture, Coach organized team building activities that encouraged us to work together and understand each other on a deeper level. One such activity was the trust fall. We had to rely on our teammates to catch us. It was an exercise in vulnerability, and as each player took their turn, we learned the value of trust and mutual support.

I remember my turn vividly. Standing with my back to the team, preparing to fall. Every muscle in my body was tense. My breathing was shallow. Coach Reynolds stood beside me.

"You have to let go," he said quietly. "Trust them."

I fell. And they caught me.

Coach Reynolds' approach was a powerful lesson in inclusivity. He wanted each of us to feel like we belonged on the team and that our contributions mattered. This inclusive atmosphere brought us closer together, making us stronger as a unit.

In the hospitality industry, building this kind of inclusive culture is essential. Employees who feel supported and valued are more motivated to deliver their best work, which positively impacts on guest satisfaction and overall team morale. When people know they belong, they invest differently. They care more. They contribute more. They stay longer.

Creating Safe Spaces for Dialogue

Effective communication is the backbone of any inclusive environment. Just as a coach encourages open discussions about team strategy, hospitality leaders should foster spaces where employees can openly share their thoughts, ideas, and concerns about inclusion.

These dialogues allow employees to express their unique perspectives and address any issues that may be affecting their experience at work. Encouraging open communication helps managers understand the diverse needs of their team members and address potential barriers to inclusion.

After difficult matches, Coach Scott would gather us in a circle and ask each person to share their perspective. What did you see? What worked? What didn't? What could we do better? There were no wrong answers. No one was dismissed or ridiculed. Every voice mattered.

This practice created psychological safety. We knew we could speak up without fear of judgment or retaliation. That safety led to better ideas, more honest feedback, and stronger team bonds.

In hospitality, creating these safe spaces might mean regular team huddles where everyone can contribute ideas, one on one check ins where employees can share concerns privately, anonymous feedback channels for sensitive issues, or diversity discussion groups where cultural differences can be explored and understood.

The key is making these spaces genuinely safe. If employees speak up and face negative consequences, safety disappears. If leaders dismiss concerns or get defensive, the dialogue shuts down. Safe spaces require leaders who listen without judgment, respond with empathy, and act when needed.

Implementing Fair and Transparent Practices

Inclusion requires more than good intentions; it requires systems and practices that ensure fairness at every level. From hiring to promotion to evaluation, processes should be consistent, transparent, and free from bias.

This means establishing clear criteria for advancement that everyone understands, using structured interviews that reduce subjective bias, reviewing compensation regularly to ensure equity across demographics, and creating accountability for inclusive practices at every level of leadership.

In soccer, the rules are the same for everyone. The field dimensions don't change based on who's playing. The scoring system is transparent. Everyone knows what they need to do to win. That fairness is essential to the integrity of the game.

The same principle applies in hospitality. When employees see that promotions are based on merit rather than favoritism, when they trust that their compensation is fair, when they believe the rules apply equally to everyone, they invest more fully in the organization. Fairness builds trust. Trust builds engagement. Engagement drives performance.

Implementing the Inclusion Play: Practical Steps

Creating an inclusive culture requires intentional effort and a commitment to fostering a supportive, diverse environment. Here are practical ways hospitality leaders can implement the Inclusion Play:

Celebrating Diversity Through Shared Experiences

Organize activities that encourage team members to share their backgrounds and unique experiences. This might include cultural potlucks where employees bring dishes from their heritage, storytelling sessions where team members share meaningful traditions, language exchange programs where employees teach each other phrases from their native languages, or heritage month celebrations that honor different cultures throughout the year. These activities help employees understand and appreciate each other's perspectives, building a sense of camaraderie and mutual respect. They transform diversity from an abstract concept into lived experience, making it tangible and valuable.

Make Inclusion a Core Value

Promote a culture of belonging by making inclusion a fundamental part of the organization's values. This isn't about lip service or corporate slogans; it's about genuine commitment demonstrated through actions.

Regularly communicate the importance of inclusivity in meetings, training, and everyday interactions. Model respectful, welcoming behavior that encourages others to do the same. Hold leaders accountable for creating inclusive teams. Recognize and reward inclusive behaviors. Make it clear that discrimination, bias, or exclusion will not be tolerated. When inclusion is treated as a core value rather than a side initiative, it permeates every aspect of the organization. It influences who gets hired, who gets promoted, how decisions get made, and how success gets defined.

Foster Open Dialogue Consistently

Create spaces (both formal and informal) where employees feel comfortable sharing their thoughts on inclusion. This might include monthly team meetings with dedicated time for open discussion, anonymous suggestion boxes for sensitive topics, small group conversations facilitated by trained leaders, or one on one check ins that include questions about inclusion and belonging.

Use these dialogues to learn about employee experiences and to implement changes that address any challenges they may be facing. Listen actively. Take notes. Follow up on concerns. Show that feedback leads to action, not just acknowledgment.

Review and Refine Practices Regularly

Ensure that hiring, promotion, and evaluation processes are consistent and transparent. Review these processes regularly to address any unintentional biases and maintain a level playing field for all employees. This might involve conducting regular pay equity audits, analyzing promotion data for demographic patterns, reviewing job descriptions for biased language, training hiring managers on unconscious bias, or creating diverse interview panels to reduce individual bias.

Fairness isn't a one-time achievement; it's an ongoing practice that requires vigilance and commitment. What seems fair at first glance might contain hidden biases. What worked five years ago might need updating. Continuous improvement in fairness demonstrates genuine commitment to inclusion.

Recognize and Celebrate Inclusive Behaviors

Acknowledge employees who contribute to building an inclusive environment. Whether through team shout outs, awards, or public recognition, celebrating inclusivity reinforces the organization's commitment to diversity and respect.

Recognize the manager who mentors employees from underrepresented groups. Celebrate the team members who speak up when they witness bias. Acknowledge the leader who creates psychological safety in their department. Reward the employee who suggests innovative ways to make the workplace more inclusive. What gets recognized gets repeated. By celebrating inclusive behaviors, you signal what matters and encourage others to follow suit.

Personal Reflection: Building an Inclusive Team

Reflecting on my journey, the lessons of inclusivity I learned from Coach Scott and Coach Reynolds were transformative. They showed me that building a strong team requires more than just technical skills; it requires respect, open mindedness, and a willingness to embrace diversity. As I entered the hospitality industry, these principles became the foundation of my leadership approach.

One of the most impactful moments came during a recruitment drive for our hotel. We had applicants from a variety of backgrounds, each bringing unique perspectives and experiences. Some had traditional hospitality education. Others came from completely different industries. Some were recent immigrants still learning English. Others had been in the country their whole lives.

Remembering Coach Scott's teachings, I focused not only on each candidate's qualifications but also on the diversity of thought they could bring to our team. I encouraged my hiring team to look beyond the traditional profile of a hospitality employee. We asked questions like: What unique perspective does this person bring? What can they teach us? How will they expand our team's capabilities?

I encouraged my hiring team to look for candidates who could add new dimensions to our service culture, knowing that a diverse team would enrich our guests' experiences. We hired a former teacher who brought exceptional training skills. We hired a military veteran who understood discipline and teamwork at a deep level. We hired a recent immigrant who could serve guests in three languages and understood cultural nuances we'd never considered.

This inclusive approach paid off beyond our expectations. Our team has become more dynamic and innovative, with employees contributing unique ideas that helped us solve challenges and enhance our guest experience. The former teacher revolutionized our training program. The veteran created systems that improved our efficiency. The multilingual employee became a bridge to international guests and helped us understand subtle cultural preferences. By fostering a culture of inclusion, we created an environment where everyone felt empowered to share their best ideas and be themselves, which strengthened our team and improved our performance. Guest satisfaction scores went up. Employee retention improved. The energy in the hotel has shifted. People wanted to work there. People wanted to stay.

More importantly, the inclusive culture we built became self-reinforcing. New employees saw that diversity was valued and felt comfortable bringing their authentic selves to work. Existing employees became more open to learning from each other. Problems got solved faster because more perspectives were contributing solutions.

The Impact of The Inclusion Play

The Inclusion Play creates a team that values every individual, building a sense of unity that enhances engagement, reduces turnover, and promotes a positive work environment. When hospitality leaders embrace inclusiveness, they not only create a supportive workplace but also drive organizational success. Just as a sports team thrives when each player feels valued and respected, a hospitality team reaches new heights when every employee feels they belong.

Building an inclusive team is an ongoing journey, one that requires dedication and intentionality. Leaders must commit to continuously learning, adapting, and fostering an environment where everyone feels respected and valued. The Inclusion Play is about creating a culture of belonging that resonates with each team member, driving them to contribute their best to the organization.

But let's be clear about what inclusion really means. It's not about being nice or politically correct. It's not about lowering standards or giving people things they haven't earned. It's not about avoiding difficult conversations or pretending differences don't exist.

Inclusion is about harnessing the full potential of every person on your team. It's about recognizing that different backgrounds, perspectives, and experiences make you stronger, not weaker. It's about creating an environment where everyone can contribute their best work because they feel safe, valued, and respected.

When Coach Scott built our diverse soccer team, he didn't lower expectations. He raised them. He expected us to learn from each other, to adapt, to grow. He expected us to perform at the highest level precisely because of our diversity, not despite it.

That's what inclusion looks like in practice. It's rigorous. It's demanding. It's excellent. And it produces results that homogeneous teams simply cannot achieve.

The Inclusion Commitment

In the end, inclusiveness isn't just a strategy; it's a mindset and a commitment to creating a team that reflects the diversity of the world. By implementing the Inclusion Play, hospitality leaders can create a workplace that celebrates every individual, fostering a cohesive team that works together to achieve greatness.

Think about the world we serve in hospitality. Guests come from every corner of the planet, speaking hundreds of languages, practicing different religions, observing different customs, expecting different things. How can we serve this diverse world effectively if our teams are homogeneous? How can we understand what guests need if we've never walked in their shoes?

We can't. At least not as well as we could with diverse, inclusive teams.

The Inclusion Play is both a moral imperative and a competitive advantage. It's the right thing to do because every person deserves respect, dignity, and opportunity. It's also the smart thing to do because diverse teams outperform, innovate better, and serve guests more effectively.

As you implement this play, remember Coach Scott standing in the Saudi heat, watching our motley crew of American, British, Canadian, and Saudi kids struggle through drills. He could have built a team of similar players with similar styles. It would have been easier, more predictable, and less complicated.

Instead, he built a team that reflected the world. A team that learned from its differences. A team that became stronger because of its diversity.

That team won championships not despite our differences but because of them.

Your team can do the same. Build it with intention. Lead it with commitment. Celebrate its diversity. Create spaces for dialogue. Ensure fairness. Recognize inclusive behaviors.

And watch what happens when everyone truly belongs.

That's the power of the Inclusion Play. That's what transforms a collection of individuals into a unified team. That's what makes hospitality not just a job but a calling where everyone can contribute, everyone can grow, and everyone can succeed. Welcome everyone to the field. Give them all a chance to play. Help them bring their best. And watch your team become something greater than you ever imagined possible.

Chapter 5: Applying Coaching techniques to the Hospitality Industry

A New Path Forward for Hospitality Leadership

Throughout my career in hospitality, I've learned that leadership isn't simply a title you earn; it's a craft you refine over time. The journey has been full of both humbling and empowering experiences, from guiding young talent to managing complex teams in high-stakes environments. Each step has brought countless lessons, some through success, many through trial and error.

But perhaps one of the most profound insights I've gained is this: true leadership is rooted in authenticity, self-assurance, and a willingness to grow alongside your team. I've witnessed firsthand how deeply the hospitality industry is affected by imposter syndrome. A sense of uncertainty often clouds the confidence of even the most capable managers. I've seen highly skilled individuals second-guess themselves, wondering if they truly belong in their roles or if they'll ever be "good enough" to lead effectively.

This lack of self-assuredness stems, in large part, from the tremendous pressure in hospitality to deliver excellence under demanding and unpredictable conditions.

Hospitality is about people and perceptions, service and satisfaction. It's an industry that requires adaptability and resourcefulness, and it can leave many managers feeling unprepared.

I remember my first month as a department head. Every decision felt enormous. Every interaction with senior leadership left me wondering if I'd said the right thing. Every mistake my team made felt like a personal failure, proof that I wasn't really qualified to be in that role. I would go home exhausted, not from the work itself, but from the constant mental effort of trying to appear confident when I felt anything but.

That feeling, I've learned, is nearly universal in hospitality leadership. We're promoted because we're good at our jobs, only to discover that managing others requires completely different skills than doing the work ourselves. The server who could handle any table becomes a supervisor who struggles to give feedback. The front desk agent who knew every guest becomes a manager who can't seem to make tough decisions. The chef who created magic in the kitchen becomes an executive who drowns in paperwork and personnel issues. The gap between competence and confidence can feel insurmountable.

The Challenge of Authentic Leadership

Imposter syndrome thrives where there is a disconnect between how people perceive themselves and how they think others perceive them. In hospitality, that disconnect can be especially intense.

Managers are often promoted based on technical skills and work experience, only to realize that leading a team requires an entirely different skill set. When they start out, many managers are overwhelmed by the complex balancing act of serving guests, meeting business targets, and inspiring team members. They may feel like they're simply playing a part, doing what they think is expected rather than trusting their instincts and embracing their unique qualities as leaders.

I once worked with a newly promoted restaurant manager who was exceptional at her job. She knew the menu inside out, could anticipate service issues before they happened, and had a natural rapport with guests. But as a manager, she struggled. She tried to be the stern, no-nonsense leader she thought she should be, even though that style felt completely foreign to her warm, collaborative nature.

Her team noticed the disconnect. They sensed she wasn't being herself. Trust eroded. Performance suffered. She was miserable.

When we finally sat down to talk about it, she broke down. "I don't know how to be a manager," she said. "I'm just pretending to be someone I'm not." That's when we had the breakthrough conversation about authenticity.

From a coaching perspective, I've found that helping managers overcome this disconnect involves nurturing their authentic selves. Authenticity, however, isn't something that comes easily; it requires confidence and a willingness to be vulnerable, qualities that aren't always encouraged in traditional leadership settings.

Yet I've come to understand that the most effective leaders are those who bring their whole selves to their work, creating an environment where their teams feel safe to do the same.

When that restaurant manager stopped trying to be someone else and started leading from her natural strengths (collaboration, warmth, clear communication), everything changed. Her team responded. Performance improved. And most importantly, she stopped feeling like a fraud.

Authenticity doesn't mean you never push yourself or that you don't grow into your role. It means you build on your strengths rather than trying to become someone else entirely. It means you acknowledge your learning curve instead of pretending you know everything. It means you lead like yourself, not like some idealized version of what you think a leader should be.

Industry Insight: Coach Scott on Character in Leadership

Years after my time playing soccer under Coach Scott, I had the opportunity to interview him about his approach to building teams. His philosophy offers powerful parallels for hospitality leadership.

"Skill is crucial, of course," Coach Scott explained, "but it's not everything. I'm looking for players who are resilient, team-oriented, and who have the kind of work ethic that pushes them to always give their best. You can train skills, but character is what makes or breaks a team."

This insight resonates deeply in hospitality. We often hire for technical competence: can someone operate the PMS system, mix drinks correctly, or fold linens to standard? But character (resilience, authenticity, team orientation) is what determines whether they'll thrive in the high-pressure environment of hospitality.

Coach Scott assesses character through observing how candidates handle pressure. "I look at how players handle pressure," he said. "Are they calm, strategic, and focused even when things aren't going well? That tells me a lot about their mindset and whether they have the mental strength to push through challenges."

This same principle applies when evaluating leadership potential in hospitality. The manager who remains authentic and composed during a system outage at check-in, a kitchen backup during dinner rush, or a guest complaint demonstrates the character necessary for sustainable leadership success. "One of the biggest red flags for me is when a player doesn't seem interested in the team's success, when it's all about them," Coach Scott explained. "I want players who celebrate their teammates' successes as much as their own."

In hospitality leadership, this translates to managers who genuinely care about developing their team members, who take pride in their staff's growth, and who understand that their success is intrinsically linked to the success of those they lead.

Moving Forward

In this chapter, I'll share the tools and lessons I've accumulated over the years: insights that I believe can make a real difference for those struggling with imposter syndrome in hospitality. I'm not here to give out quick fixes or shortcuts; rather, I want to share the practices, mental frameworks, and strategies that have helped me and others build confidence, embrace feedback, and grow into our roles.

The journey toward authentic, effective leadership in hospitality requires both internal work and external systems.

It demands that we address our own imposter syndrome while simultaneously building the structures (hiring processes, feedback mechanisms, conflict resolution protocols) that allow our teams to thrive.

Think about Coach Scott standing on that field in Saudi Arabia. After every game, he'd gather us to review what happened. He'd point out mistakes, sure. But he never made those mistakes, which meant we were failures. He made them mean we had opportunities to get better.

"You left the near post exposed on that corner kick. Let's work on your positioning this week. "Not: "You're a terrible goalkeeper."

The difference is everything. That's the kind of leadership hospitality needs: authentic, growth-oriented, and grounded in the reality that we're all learning, all the time.

Understanding the Specific Needs of Your Hospitality Business

Here's the truth nobody wants to admit: **that rockstar server who crushed it at the downtown bistro? They might completely flame out at your resort property.** And that front desk agent who was pure gold at your budget hotel? They could be totally wrong for your boutique luxury brand.

I learned this lesson the hard way twenty years ago when I hired what I thought was a "hospitality professional" – someone with a stellar resume and great references. Two weeks in, they were miserable, the team was frustrated, and I was wondering what I'd missed. What I'd missed was simple: I never asked myself what _my specific operation_ needed.

Your property isn't a template. Your hiring shouldn't be either.

Let's start with your operational environment, because it matters more than most people realize:

Luxury vs. Budget: If you're running a five-star property, you need people who can anticipate needs three steps ahead, who understand the art of invisible service, and who won't blink when a guest asks for something ridiculous at 2 AM. Budget properties? You need efficiency experts, people who can juggle ten tasks simultaneously without missing a beat, and who can deliver warmth and competence even when they're understaffed. Neither is "better." They're just completely different skill sets.

F&B vs. Rooms Division: Restaurant operations move at a different tempo than front office work. In F&B, you need people who thrive in controlled chaos, who can read a dining room like a book, and who understand that timing isn't just important. It's everything. Rooms division requires people who can maintain composure during long shifts, who excel at problem solving on the fly, and who can be both the first smile and the last impression a guest receives. If you're hiring for both, recognize that the same person might not excel in both arenas.

Urban vs. Resort: Urban properties attract people who want fast paced, high volume environments with guests who often know exactly what they want. Resort properties need team members who can be entertainment directors, concierges, and therapists all at once... people who build relationships over a guest's weeklong stay. The personality types are often opposite.

Now, **dig into your guest demographic and their expectations.** Are you serving business travelers who value efficiency over personality? Families who need patience and flexibility? Wealthy retirees who expect white glove service? Instagram obsessed millennials who'll forgive slow service if the ambiance is perfect? Your ideal hire needs to *naturally* connect with whoever walks through your doors.

I always tell people: spend a week watching your operation with fresh eyes. **What are the moments that make or break the guest experience at YOUR property?** For one of my restaurant clients, it was the sixty second window when guests first sat down. That's when the entire vibe was established. For a resort I worked with, it was the late-night moments when the main lobby had quietened down, and guests felt comfortable asking for help with real problems. Figure out your moments, then hire people who can own those moments.

Your turn. Before you write another job post, answer these questions:

- What are the top three challenges that break new hires at our property?
- What personality traits do our best current employees share?
- What do guests complain about most, and which employee skills would prevent those complaints?
- What's our biggest operational bottleneck, and who could solve it?

Write these answers down. Seriously, write them down. Because these answers become your hiring blueprint.

Creating an Interview Guide with a Purpose to Keep You on Track

Let me tell you about the worst interview I ever conducted. I sat down with a candidate, had what I thought was a "great conversation," and hired them on the spot. Three months later, they were gone. When I reviewed my notes (what few I'd taken), I realized I'd spent forty-five minutes talking about college football and about fifteen minutes discussing the job. I had no idea what I'd learned about them as an employee. I just knew they were Michigan fans.

An interview guide saved my career.

Not a script. I'm not asking you to become a robot. But a structured roadmap that ensures you evaluate what matters instead of just enjoying the conversation. Here's how to build one that works:

Start with your non-negotiables. Based on that work you did in the previous section, identify the 5 to 7 skills or attributes that someone MUST have to succeed in your environment. For a high-volume breakfast restaurant, that might be speed, multitasking, grace under pressure, early morning reliability, and team coordination. For a luxury hotel front desk: discretion, problem solving, verbal polish, technology comfort, and emotional regulation.

Each of these non-negotiables gets 2 to 3 dedicated questions in your guide.

Build consistency into your process. This is where most people roll their eyes but stick with me. You're not creating consistency to check some HR box. You're doing it because it's the only way to compare candidates. If you ask Sarah about dealing with difficult guests but ask Tom about his favorite part of hospitality, you can't compare their customer service skills. You're comparing apples to inspirational quotes.

Your guide should have:

- **Opening questions** (same for everyone) to establish rapport
- **Core competency questions** (same for everyone) that map to your non-negotiables
- **Role specific questions** (same for everyone applying for that specific position)
- **Flexibility space** for follow up questions based on their answers

Navigate legal compliance without becoming a compliance officer. Look, I'm not a lawyer, and you probably aren't either. But your interview guide protects you by keeping you focused on job related questions. Here's the simple rule: every question should be something you'd ask *everyone* applying for that role, and every question should relate to performing the job.

Don't ask: "Do you have kids?" or "Where are you from?" or "What does your spouse do?"

Do ask: "This position requires weekend and evening availability. Does that work with your schedule?" or "We're a fast-paced environment with shifting priorities. Tell me about a time you handled multiple urgent demands."

See the difference? You get the information you need (availability, adaptability) without stumbling into protected territory.

Use your guide to compare objectively. After each interview, score responses to your core questions on a simple scale (1 to 5 works fine). This isn't about reducing humans to numbers. It's about forcing yourself to evaluate what you heard, not just how you felt. I've watched myself fall for charismatic candidates who gave terrible answers to important questions. The scoring system made me see reality. Suddenly, you can see patterns. You can make decisions based on your actual needs, not just who you like chatting with.

Pro tip: Keep your interview guide in a shared document that your whole hiring team can access. When three managers interview candidates, everyone asks the same core questions. Then you can discuss what you learned rather than just sharing feelings. Your interview guide isn't a constraint. It's your insurance policy against expensive hiring mistakes.

Behavioral Interview Questions

(Lesson from the Bleachers)

I learned my greatest interviewing lesson watching my daughter's softball coach evaluate new players. Instead of asking "Are you a good teammate?" he'd say, "Tell me about a game where your team was losing badly. What did you do?"

The difference in answers was stunning. Some kids talked about encouraging their teammates. Others admitted they sulked. A few described analyzing what was going wrong and suggesting adjustments. He learned more in two minutes than most coaches learned in a week of practice.

That's the power of behavioral interview questions.

Here's why hypothetical questions fail in hospitality: everyone knows the "right" answer. "How would you handle an angry guest?" "Oh, I'd listen carefully, show empathy, and solve their problem. "Great. That's what everyone says. What did you learn?

Behavioral questions force candidates to show you their real patterns. Because unless someone is a truly gifted liar, they can't fake their way through a detailed story about something they experienced.

Instead ask: **"Tell me about the angriest guest you've ever dealt with. Walk me through what happened and what you did."**

Now you're getting somewhere. You'll hear:

- How they read situations
- Where their instincts take them
- Whether they take ownership or blame others
- How they solve problems under pressure
- What they consider a "successful" resolution

The framework is simple: STAR

- **Situation:** What was the context?
- **Task:** What needed to be done?
- **Action:** What did YOU specifically do?
- **Result:** What happened?

But here's where most people screw this up: they accept surface level answers.

Candidate: "I once had a guest who was upset about their room. I listened to them and got them a new room. They were happy."

You: *thinking this is a great answer and moving on*

WRONG. You just learned almost nothing. Dig deeper:

You: "Tell me more about what they were upset about specifically."

You: "What made you decide on a new room was the right solution?"

You: "Walk me through the conversation. What did you say?"

You: "How did you handle this while managing your other responsibilities?"

You: "What did you learn from this that you've used since?" See how much more you get? The follow up questions reveal competence, judgment, values, and learning ability.

Here is my battle tested behavioral questions for hospitality:

For Customer Service Excellence:

- "Describe a time when you had to tell a guest 'No' or that you couldn't give them what they wanted. How did you handle it?"

- "Tell me about a time you recovered from a situation where a guest had a genuinely bad experience."
- "Give me an example of when you went beyond your job description to help a guest."

For Handling Pressure:

- "Walk me through the most chaotic shift you've ever worked. What was happening and how did you manage?"
- "Tell me about a time everything seemed to go wrong at once. What did you do first?"
- "Describe a situation where you were completely overwhelmed. How did you get through it?"

For Team Dynamics:

- "Tell me about a time you had a conflict with a coworker. What caused it and what happened?"
- "Give me an example of when you had to depend on teammates who weren't pulling their weight. How did you handle it?"
- "Describe a time you helped train or support a struggling colleague."

For Problem Solving:

- "Tell me about a time you had to solve a problem without manager assistance. What was the problem and what did you do?"
- "Describe a situation where you broke a rule or standard procedure because you thought it was the right thing to do."
- "Walk me through a time when you failed at something at work. What happened and what did you learn?"

What to listen for:

Ownership vs. Blame. Do they say "I" or "we"? Do they take responsibility or point fingers? In their stories, are they the hero who saved the day or the victim of circumstances?

Specificity. Vague answers like "I always" or "I usually" are red flags. Real experiences have details.

Learning and growth. Do they reflect on what they learned? Do past experiences change future behavior?

Values alignment. Do their instincts match your culture? If they describe "winning" an argument with a guest, and your culture is about hospitality first service recovery, you've got a mismatch.

Consistency. Are the same themes appearing across multiple answers? If every story involves conflict with coworkers, pay attention.

I'll share my favorite behavioral question from a legendary hotel GM I know:

"Tell me about a time you broke a guest's trust, even accidentally. What happened?"

It's brilliant because it assumes imperfection (everyone has messed up) and asks for vulnerability. The way candidates respond to this tells you everything about their integrity, accountability, and self-awareness.

If they can't think of an example? That's not a good sign. Either they're lying, they lack self-awareness, or they've never taken enough ownership to realize when they fell short.

Becoming a Mentalist of Behaviors

Alright, let's talk about the part of interviewing that nobody wants to admit matters: **your gut.**

I know, I know. I just spent three sections telling you to be structured and objective. And all that stands. But there's another layer here... the ability to read what's happening beneath the words. To sense when something's off. To trust your instincts while remaining fair.

The best interviewers are part investigator, part psychologist, and part detective.

Let's start with body language, but not the pseudo-science version. Forget the myths about crossed arms meaning someone's defensive (maybe they're just cold) or lack of eye contact meaning they're lying (maybe they're neurodivergent or from a culture where direct eye contact is disrespectful).

What you're looking for are patterns and incongruencies.

Watch for **alignment between words and body.** If someone says "I loved that job" but their whole face tightens and their shoulders drop, something's off. If they say "I work well under pressure" but they're fidgeting and can't maintain a steady voice while describing a high-pressure situation, pay attention.

Notice **energy shifts.** When do they light up? When do they deflate? I once interviewed someone who was flat and monotone throughout the entire interview until I asked about teamwork. Suddenly they were animated, specifically, smiling. That told me everything about where their passion lived.

Watch **how they treat people who "don't matter."** How do they interact with the person who escorts them to your office? Are they courteous to the front desk? Do they acknowledge housekeeping in the hallway? I've made hiring decisions based on watching candidates in the lobby before the formal interview even started.

But here's the thing about body language: context is everything. Someone who's nervous in an interview isn't necessarily a nervous employee. Someone who's confident in an interview might be a disaster on the floor. Use body language as a data point, not a decision maker.

Identifying patterns in responses is where the real skill lives.

Listen for **recurring themes.** If every story involves them solving problems alone, they might struggle with collaboration. If every conflict ends with "then I left that job," you're looking at someone who exits rather than resolves. If they never mention guests or customers in their stories, they might be task focused rather than service focused.

Pay attention to **what's missing.** If you ask about teamwork and they only talk about leading teams, they might struggle as a team member. If you ask about dealing with difficult situations and they claim to never really have any, they're either lying or they lack self-awareness.

Notice **language choices.** Do they say "guests" or "customers" or just "people"? Do they talk about "we" or "I"? Do they use industry language correctly or are they faking familiarity? Are they blaming external factors or taking ownership?

Spotting red flags early:

The story that's too perfect. Real experiences are messy. If every story ends with applause and promotion, something's off.

Badmouthing previous employers. One toxic workplace? Okay. Three toxic workplaces? The common denominator is them.

Inability to discuss failures or weaknesses. Everyone has them. Someone who can't admit theirs, lacks self-awareness.

Overconfidence about things they haven't done. "I've never worked a double shift but I'm sure I could handle it easily" is different from "I've never worked a double, but I'm used to long hours from..."

Inconsistencies. They say they love fast paced environments but describe being happiest during slow shifts. They claim they're a morning person but mention sleeping multiple times.

Treating the interview like a formality. If they're not asking thoughtful questions about the role, they're either desperate or not really interested. Both are problems.

Now, here's the controversial part: trusting your instincts.

I've hired people who looked perfect on paper and something in my gut said no. I ignored it. They were disasters. I've hired people who had gaps in their resume and quirks in their interview, but something about them felt *right*. They became stars.

Your instincts are pattern recognition software built from years of experience. They're picking up micro signals you can't consciously articulate. **But instincts alone are dangerous.** They can be biased, they can be based on irrelevant factors like attractiveness or similarity to you, they can be flat wrong.

So, here's the balance:

Use your structure and objectivity as the foundation. Score the responses. Compare the candidates fairly.

Then ask yourself: **"Does something feel off that I can't explain?"**

If yes, dig deeper. Don't reject them based on a feeling. Use that feeling as a signal to ask more questions, check references more thoroughly, maybe add another interview.

Also ask: **"Am I drawn to this person for reasons unrelated to the job?"**

Are they charming? Attractive? Similar to you? From your alma mater? These are bias red flags. Make sure you can objectively justify your enthusiasm.

The mentalist's toolkit:

The long pause. After they answer a question, stay silent for 3 to 4 seconds. Most people will fill that silence with additional information, often the real information.

The echo technique. Repeat the last few words they said as a question. "You decided to leave after that?" They'll often expand in revealing ways.

The hypothetical follows up. After a behavioral question, ask: "If that situation happened today, would you do anything differently?" This shows growth and learning ability.

The pattern call out. "I'm noticing that in several of your stories, you mention stepping away from teams to work independently. Tell me more about that." Forces self-awareness and honest self-assessment.

The reference question. "When I call your references, what will they tell me where your greatest strengths? What will they say you could improve?" Then actually check if the reference call matches their prediction.

Look, at the end of the day, **hiring is part science, part art.** The structure keeps you honest. Instinct keeps you human. Use both.

A hotel industry legend once told me: "**I hire for the gut check, but I fire for ignoring the red flags.**" What he meant was this: when someone felt right *and* demonstrated competence, they thrived. But when he ignored warning signs because he liked someone, it always came back to bite him.

Be a mentalist. Be objective. And be honest with yourself about what you're seeing.

The perfect hire is out there. Your job is to see them when they walk in the door.

The Eight Non-Coachable Behaviors

Understanding what you cannot coach is just as important as knowing what you can develop. As you interview candidates and observe your existing team, these eight behaviors should serve as red flags. While technical skills can be taught and soft skills can be developed, these fundamental character issues are extraordinarily difficult, if not impossible, to change through coaching.

Recognizing these behaviors early, whether in the hiring process or during performance management, can save you months of frustration and protect your team's culture.

Industry Insight: Coach Scott on Identifying Red Flags

When I asked Coach Scott how he spots un-coachable behaviors during tryouts, his response was illuminating: "I watch how they respond to correction. Do they adjust, or do they make excuses? Do they blame their teammates, or do they own their part? Those early signals tell me everything I need to know about whether someone is coachable."

This wisdom applies directly to hospitality hiring. During working interviews or trial shifts, observe not just what candidates do, but how they respond when things don't go perfectly.

1. Arrogant: Feeling of Entitlement

Addressing arrogance and feelings of entitlement within a team requires a coach's commitment to building humility and respect among members, as arrogance can quickly disrupt team dynamics and breed resentment. From a coach's perspective, the first step in tackling these behaviors is recognizing the signs, which might include dismissing team input, monopolizing discussions, or expecting preferential treatment. Such actions can make others feel undervalued and diminish the collective spirit, which is essential for any high-performing team.

In sports, a player who disregards a coach's instructions or fails to acknowledge teammates' contributions on the field may demonstrate entitlement, expecting that their skills alone will carry the game. A coach observing this behavior would be wise to step in early, as unchecked entitlement not only alienates teammates but also impacts overall performance. Similarly, in the workplace, when a team member consistently overrides colleagues' ideas or expects special treatment, it disrupts harmony and weakens trust within the group.

One of the most effective ways to address entitlement is through candid, constructive feedback. A coach wouldn't simply ignore a player's arrogant behavior; instead, they would call attention to it respectfully and provide context for why humility and teamwork are non-negotiable values. In a workplace setting, a manager might address entitlement by having a private conversation where the behavior is discussed openly. For example, a manager could say, "I've noticed that in meetings, you sometimes dismiss your colleagues' ideas before they fully explain them. It's essential for everyone to feel heard, as each person's perspective contributes to our success." By addressing the specific behavior, the manager clarifies the issue without resorting to personal criticism, reinforcing the idea that every team member's input is valuable.

Another important aspect of addressing entitlement is setting clear expectations around behavior and teamwork. A coach establishes guidelines that emphasize the importance of humility, encouraging players to put the team's needs above personal recognition. In the workplace, managers can reinforce these expectations by communicating the importance of mutual respect, open-mindedness, and shared accountability.

In some cases, entitlement may stem from a lack of self-awareness, where individuals may not realize how their actions affect others. A coach knows that awareness is the first step toward behavioral change and will often work with players to help them see themselves through the eyes of their teammates. Similarly, in the workplace, managers can use specific examples to illustrate the impact of an employee's behavior.

Role modeling is also a powerful tool for addressing entitlement, as it shows employees how humility and respect look in action. A coach sets the tone by demonstrating teamwork, acknowledging players' efforts, and listening to feedback, creating an environment where entitlement has no place.

If entitlement persists despite these efforts, managers may need to implement more structured interventions, such as setting specific behavioral goals within a Performance Improvement Plan (PIP). A coach who sees repeated arrogance in a player might require them to complete specific teamwork-related tasks. In the workplace, a PIP can similarly outline behavioral objectives that address entitlement directly.

Throughout this process, it's essential for managers to remain empathetic and patient, as changing ingrained behaviors like entitlement can take time. However, if the behavior continues to poison team culture, the courageous decision may be to remove the individual from the team entirely.

2. Lack of Empathy

Approaching a lack of empathy from a coach's perspective in hospitality requires a deep understanding of human behavior and interpersonal relationships. Imagine a skilled player on a sports team who excels in individual performance but fails to connect emotionally with teammates, often ignoring their struggles or expressing impatience. On the field, this player's lack of empathy causes friction; they might show frustration when a teammate makes an error or fail to offer support during a challenging play. This behavior disrupts the team dynamic, leading others to feel isolated or undervalued.

In hospitality, an employee with similar tendencies might become impatient with a colleague under pressure during a busy shift, showing little understanding of the stress that person may be experiencing. This lack of empathy not only lowers morale but impacts on the team's ability to function as a unified force. Coaching empathy in both sports and hospitality is challenging because empathy is not a skill easily taught or measured like technical skills. It requires a shift in mindset, a way of connecting with others, and an ability to see beyond one's own perspective. In sports, a coach may start by helping the player recognize their behavior's impact on the team. One approach is to create opportunities for perspective-shifting. In hospitality, this might involve role-play or simulations where employees switch roles, such as a front-of-house team member experiencing a back-of-house role during peak hours. By stepping into each other's shoes, they start to understand the challenges each position entails, cultivating a sense of respect and patience.

To further foster empathy, structured exercises and training sessions focused on active listening and cultural sensitivity can be invaluable. Hospitality settings are diverse, with staff often hailing from various cultural backgrounds, each bringing their unique perspectives and communication styles. An empathetic team member needs to understand and respect these differences to work harmoniously.

However, the hard truth is this: while you can create conditions that encourage empathy, you cannot force someone who fundamentally lacks this quality to develop it. Some people, despite all efforts, remain unable or unwilling to connect emotionally with others. In hospitality, where guest service depends on genuine care and connection, a complete lack of empathy is a disqualifying trait.

3. No Removal of Guilt: The Blame Shifter

In both sports and hospitality, fostering a culture of accountability is essential for team success. From a coach's perspective, the challenge lies in guiding individuals who frequently blame others, deny responsibility, or even fabricate stories to avoid guilt.

Imagine a soccer player who, after a game, repeatedly points fingers at teammates for missed passes, misplaced shots, or lapses in defense. This player might be skilled, but their tendency to shift blame is evident in post-game conversations and team debriefs. They avoid eye contact when coaches review plays, sidestep direct questions about mistakes, and subtly or overtly criticize others' performances rather than reflecting on their own.

Similarly, in a hospitality setting, an employee who blames colleagues for errors (whether it's a missed guest request, a delay in service, or a room mix-up) can undermine team morale. Consider a front-desk agent who regularly deflects responsibility when a customer complaint arises. When a guest's room is not ready, they might say, "Housekeeping didn't give me the room status on time," or "The system was slow, it's not my fault." They might even subtly imply that the guest is partly to blame for arriving early.

Addressing these attitudes requires setting a clear standard from the start. A coach or manager must first communicate the importance of responsibility as a core value, framing it not as an arbitrary rule but as a foundation for personal and professional growth.

One-on-one conversations are often necessary to directly address blame-shifting behaviors. A coach working with a player who refuses to take responsibility for mistakes might begin by discussing the impact of the behavior on team dynamics.

For instance, the coach might say, "I noticed that during post-game feedback, you often focus on others' mistakes rather than reflecting on your own. Team success comes when everyone is willing to own their part. Let's talk about some areas where you could improve."

Sometimes, setting concrete expectations and consequences can be useful when dealing with individuals who consistently deflect blame. In sports, a coach might establish a rule that every player should identify one personal area of improvement after each game. This practice forces the player to think about their own actions and discourages the tendency to blame others.

In both cases, empathy plays a role in addressing accountability issues. Often, individuals who deflect blame do so out of a fear of failure or judgment. They may worry that admitting mistakes will lower others' opinions of them or lead to punitive consequences. A coach or manager can address this by fostering a supportive atmosphere, one that reassures individuals that mistakes are learning opportunities, not marks of inadequacy.

Ultimately, fostering accountability in those resistant to it requires patience, consistency, and a nuanced approach. However, if someone chronically refuses to take responsibility for their actions, continuing to employ them sends a message to the entire team that accountability is optional, and that's a message no hospitality operation can afford to send.

4. Irresponsible/Self-Destructive

Addressing irresponsible or self-destructive behaviors in a player or employee presents a significant challenge for any coach or manager. Such behaviors can stem from a range of underlying issues, from lack of self-awareness to personal struggles that spill into the professional sphere.

In the world of sports, a player exhibiting irresponsible or self-destructive tendencies may avoid practice, disregard health guidelines, or ignore team rules. They might turn up late for training sessions, dismiss coach feedback, or even engage in risky behaviors off the field that compromise their fitness and focus.

In a hospitality setting, an employee exhibiting similar behaviors might frequently miss shifts, show up unprepared, or fail to complete assigned tasks. They might call in sick more often than necessary, engage in conflicts with colleagues, or display a negative attitude that affects team morale and guest experience. For example, a front-desk agent who regularly arrives late, without proper grooming, or doesn't follow up on important guest requests can disrupt the smooth flow of operations.

As a coach, the first step in addressing these behaviors is to observe and assess. A key part of this involves understanding the motivations or circumstances driving the behavior. Is the player or employee acting out due to stress, personal issues, or lack of motivation? Or is their behavior stemming from a deeper feeling of disengagement?

Once the underlying issues have been identified, the next step is to provide the appropriate resources and support. In sports, a player dealing with personal struggles might benefit from the guidance of a sports psychologist or mental health counselor. In the hospitality industry, an employee displaying self-destructive tendencies might also benefit from similar support systems, such as an Employee Assistance

Program (EAP) that provides counseling and mental health services.

At times, structured intervention may be necessary, especially when repeated conversations and support mechanisms fail to produce meaningful changes. In sports, a coach might implement a behavior improvement plan, setting clear expectations and consequences for a player's actions.

Coaching or managing someone who displays irresponsible or self-destructive tendencies is no easy task. These behaviors are often deep-seated and may reflect underlying patterns or habits that are resistant to change. Coaches and managers need to exercise patience, recognizing that setbacks may occur and progress might be slow.

However, there comes a point where continued patience becomes enabling. When an employee's self-destructive behavior consistently impacts operations, guest experience, or team morale despite interventions and support, the responsible decision is to end the employment relationship. The team's collective well-being cannot be sacrificed for one individual's inability to function responsibly in their role.

5. Thrives and Lives for Drama

In the hospitality industry, managing an employee who thrives on drama presents a unique challenge. Drama in the workplace can manifest in various ways: an employee might indulge in gossip, spread rumors, or subtly instigate tension among colleagues. Such behaviors can be especially damaging in a customer-facing environment like hospitality, where the focus should be on delivering seamless service.

For example, imagine a front-desk agent who consistently gossips about co-workers, speculates about management decisions, or expresses negative opinions about team members to others. Their behavior can create an atmosphere of distrust and resentment among colleagues, making it difficult for team members to rely on one another.

From a coach's viewpoint, dealing with an employee who thrives on drama begins with observing and understanding the scope of the behavior. Drama can be subtle and might not always be immediately visible, but its effects are usually felt by those involved. One of the first steps a coach can take is setting clear expectations for professional behavior. This includes communicating directly with the employees about the impact of their actions and the importance of maintaining a respectful, collaborative work environment.

For a coaching approach to be effective, it's also crucial to provide specific examples of the problematic behavior rather than making generalized statements. For example, a coach might say, "Last week, I overheard you discussing another team member's personal challenges in a way that didn't seem supportive. Such conversations can create unnecessary tension and lead others to feel uncomfortable."

However, it's not enough to merely point out the behavior. A coach must also encourage positive alternatives, teaching the employee how to redirect their energy in a way that contributes to team cohesion rather than division.

Despite the coach's best efforts, some employees may struggle to change deeply ingrained habits related to drama and conflict. When progress is slow or resistance is evident, the coach may need to implement a more structured intervention, such as a performance improvement plan (PIP).

In some cases, drama-prone employees may not fully realize the extent of their behavior's impact on the team. As a coach, it's beneficial to facilitate team-building activities that highlight the importance of unity and collective purpose. For an employee accustomed to thriving on drama, the journey to becoming a constructive team member can be challenging.

They may need time to unlearn old habits, develop self-awareness, and cultivate emotional intelligence. As a coach, one must recognize that this process is gradual and requires patience and persistence.

Ultimately, the goal is to guide the employee toward a mindset that values professionalism and mutual respect, helping them understand that their behavior impacts not only their own success but also the success of their colleagues. If they prove unable or unwilling to make this shift, they have no place in a high-performing hospitality team.

Industry Insight: Coach Eberbach on Team Culture

In my conversation with Coach Eberbach, he emphasized the critical importance of team culture in preventing toxic behaviors from taking root.

"Every team needs to understand not only what they're doing but why they're doing it," he explained. "When players know their purpose, it translates into a stronger drive on the field. They're not just following instructions; they're motivated by a deeper understanding of the 'why.'"

For Coach Eberbach, building trust and unity among team members is foundational to creating a high-performing team. "You can't push someone to their potential unless they know you care about them as a person," he said. He makes it a point to know his players personally: their strengths, challenges, and aspirations. "Every player brings their own story to the field. When you acknowledge that, you can motivate them in ways that resonate deeply."

This focus on the emotional connection extends to how he handles setbacks and challenges. Rather than placing blame, he emphasizes resilience and collective growth, creating a safe space where players can learn from their mistakes without fear of criticism. "Mistakes are part of the journey," he explained. "The real test is how you bounce back and what you learn."

In hospitality, this same approach prevents drama and dysfunction from taking root. When team members feel genuinely connected to the mission, cared for as individuals, and safe to make mistakes, the appeal of gossip and drama diminishes significantly. The culture itself becomes the inoculation against toxicity.

6. Brags About Outsmarting

Addressing an employee who brags about outsmarting others can be particularly challenging for a coach, as such behavior directly undermines team cohesion and trust. From a coaching perspective, this behavior reflects a fundamental misalignment with the values of integrity, honesty, and respect that are essential for a successful team.

In hospitality, an employee who brags about deceiving others (be it colleagues, customers, or management) can severely impact the team's morale and, in turn, customer service quality. Imagine a hotel receptionist who prides themselves on charging extra fees without informing guests, or a team member who cleverly shifts their workload onto others without their awareness. This "outsmarting" may be celebrated as a personal victory by the employee, but it ultimately breeds resentment among colleagues, damages the organization's reputation, and could lead to a toxic work environment.

The first step in addressing this issue is direct, transparent communication. A coach should privately meet with the employee to discuss their behavior, providing specific examples that demonstrate how their actions have been observed and interpreted.

Much like coaching a player who boasts about bending the rules to gain an advantage, a hospitality manager must make it clear that integrity is non-negotiable. In sports, a coach might tell a player that while creativity and strategy are encouraged, honesty and sportsmanship are the core of good teamwork and success. The same principle applies in hospitality.

A key strategy in addressing this behavior is to reinforce ethical standards and values, not just in words but through clear actions and policies. It's essential to ensure that employees understand that honesty and transparency are core organizational values, and there are established consequences for actions that violate these principles.

To create a pathway for improvement, the coach should focus on redirecting the employee's desire for accomplishment towards positive goals. Many individuals who engage in this type of behavior are driven by a need for recognition, power, or a sense of superiority. A coach can channel this drive by setting clear, constructive goals that challenge the employee in ways that build both their skills and their character.

Providing opportunities for personal development is also essential in fostering a culture of integrity. Offering training on ethical decision-making and emotional intelligence can equip the employee with the tools they need to make better choices and to recognize the value of honesty and transparency.

In cases where the employee shows resistance or a lack of progress, the coach must be prepared to take further action. This might involve formal disciplinary measures or, in some cases, termination if the behavior continues to disrupt the team's integrity and morale.

The simple truth: An employee who takes pride in deceiving others (guests, colleagues, or management) has no place in hospitality. Our industry is built on trust, and one person who openly brags about manipulating that trust can destroy what takes years to build.

7. Has Short-Term Relationships: "I'm Not Here to Make Friends"

Approaching an employee who operates with an "I'm not here to make friends" mindset presents a unique challenge for a coach. In hospitality, teamwork, collaboration, and mutual support form the backbone of a successful and productive environment. Employees who resist building connections or seem uninterested in forming lasting relationships with colleagues may perform adequately in their tasks, but they often miss out on a deeper connection to the team, which is essential for cohesion, morale, and long-term success.

In the hospitality industry, where teamwork is paramount, an employee who treats every interaction as purely transactional can create a cold, detached atmosphere. Imagine a front-desk worker who views each guest's interaction as just another transaction to complete, or a server who sees working with kitchen staff as a temporary necessity rather than a valuable relationship. These employees may have the skills to fulfill their roles technically, but without deeper connections, they risk becoming isolated, which can diminish morale and reduce engagement with the team's larger goals.

A coach can begin by recognizing that the employee's approach might stem from prior experiences where workplace relationships didn't yield positive outcomes. Some employees may have encountered environments where friendships were discouraged, where competition was intense, or where they were let down by colleagues. A coach should approach this employee with empathy, understanding that they may have developed this mindset as a defense mechanism.

After opening this line of communication, a coach can then highlight the benefits of building strong relationships within the team. Just as in sports, where a coach emphasizes that players need to understand each other's strengths and play styles to succeed, hospitality professionals must develop rapport with colleagues to ensure smooth, effective service.

One effective way to promote relationship-building is to assign the employee to a collaborative project that requires teamwork and communication. For example, in a hotel setting, the coach could assign them a task that requires working closely with different departments, such as front desk, housekeeping, and guest services.

Team-building activities can also serve as valuable tools for cultivating relationships. While some employees may initially resist such activities, viewing them as forced or superficial, well-designed exercises can reveal how collaboration enriches the work environment.

It's also essential to provide ongoing encouragement and support for relationship-building in daily operations. Coaches can make a point of celebrating examples of teamwork, reinforcing the idea that individual achievements are less impactful than collective success.

For employees with an "I'm not here to make friends" attitude, it can also be effective to frame relationship-building as a professional skill rather than a social obligation. In hospitality, where guest experience is paramount, the ability to work harmoniously with others impacts not only internal dynamics but also the quality of service provided.

Challenges are inevitable when guiding an employee to shift from a transactional mindset to a collaborative one, and a coach must be prepared for gradual progress rather than immediate change. The coach should also clearly outline the organization's expectations regarding teamwork and collaboration in performance evaluations.

However, here's the reality: while you don't need to be best friends with your colleagues, you absolutely must be willing to build professional relationships based on trust and mutual respect. An employee who actively resists connection with their team will never fully contribute to the collaborative environment that hospitality demands. If someone genuinely cannot or will not work on building positive relationships with teammates, they're fundamentally incompatible with hospitality work.

8. Fantasy World: Delusional About How Everyone Else Perceives Their Reality

Addressing an individual who lives in a "fantasy world" or is delusional about how others perceive them is a delicate and complex challenge for any coach, whether they're guiding a player on a sports team or an employee in a professional environment. Such individuals are often convinced of their own effectiveness and positive image, ignoring or misinterpreting feedback that suggests otherwise. This detachment from reality can harm team dynamics, as the person's inflated self-perception may create friction, frustration, or a lack of trust among teammates.

From a coach's perspective, dealing with a player or employee in this situation begins with understanding the root causes of their disconnection from reality. People who exhibit such behaviors often have underlying insecurities, fears, or past experiences that have shaped their self-image. They might overestimate their abilities as a way to shield themselves from self-doubt or criticism.

The first step in addressing this issue is to create a safe environment for open and honest conversations. For example, imagine a player who believes they're performing at a level that far surpasses reality. They may disregard constructive feedback from teammates or the coach, convinced they are making critical contributions even when they're consistently underperforming.

When providing feedback to an individual detached from reality, specificity is essential. Broad statements or general critiques will likely be dismissed or misunderstood. The coach should focus on specific instances where the player's self-perception has clashed with feedback from the team. In parallel, it's essential to engage the player or employee in self-assessment exercises. By encouraging them to reflect on their actions and consider their impact, the coach can gradually help them bridge the gap between their perception and reality.

Additionally, team dynamics play a critical role in addressing a player or employee's detachment from reality. In some cases, an individual's unrealistic self-perception may alienate their peers, creating friction or resentment. As a coach, it's crucial to facilitate open communication within the team, encouraging mutual respect and constructive dialogue.

One practical method to realign the individual's self-perception is to set measurable goals and track their progress over time. For example, if a player believes they're an excellent shooter but consistently misses key shots, the coach might establish a shooting accuracy goal for the player to work toward. By tracking their performance with concrete data, the player receives undeniable evidence of their abilities, which helps adjust their perception. Throughout this process, patience and consistency are vital. People who live in a fantasy world often need time to process feedback and adjust their self-perception. A coach may need to have several discussions with the individual, reinforcing the same points and providing additional examples as necessary.

As the individual begins to accept feedback and adjust their self-image, the coach can reinforce positive behaviors and celebrate milestones. The ultimate goal is to guide the individual toward a balanced self-awareness, where they understand both their strengths and areas for improvement.

However, if someone remains fundamentally unable to see themselves accurately despite repeated, specific feedback and measurable performance data, they cannot function effectively in a team environment. Their delusional self-perception will continue to alienate teammates and undermine trust, making them uncoachable and ultimately unsuitable for the role.

The Bottom Line on Un-Coachable Behaviors

As coaches, our ultimate mission is to bring out the best in our players or employees, guiding them toward success while ensuring that the team as a whole thrives. Performance management, in any context, is akin to the playbook every successful coach needs. It's the framework that ensures players have the skills, discipline, and attitude necessary to deliver consistent results.

However, the eight behaviors outlined above represent fundamental character issues that resist coaching. While we can teach technical skills, develop soft skills, and mentor growth mindsets, we cannot fundamentally change someone's character when they:

- Feel entitled to special treatment
- Lack empathy for others
- Refuse to take responsibility
- Engage in self-destructive behaviors
- Create drama constantly
- Pride themselves on deceiving others
- Refuse to build professional relationships
- Cannot see themselves as others see them

Recognizing these behaviors during the interview process (or addressing them swiftly when they emerge in existing team members) is not about giving up on people. It's about protecting your team culture, maintaining operational excellence, and being honest about the limits of coaching.

Every person you bring onto your team either lifts the entire group up or drags them down. There is no neutral. When you identify un-coachable behaviors, you're not making a judgment about someone's worth as a human being. You're making a professional assessment about their fit for your team and your operation.

And sometimes, the most compassionate thing you can do (for them, for your team, and for yourself) is to make the difficult decision quickly and clearly.

Integrating New Hires into the Team and Setting Them Up for Success

Here's a stat that should terrify you: **most hospitality employees decide whether they're staying or leaving within their first two weeks.** Not two months. Two weeks.

And here's the kicker... it's usually not about the job itself. It's about how we welcome them. Or more accurately, how we don't.

I watched this play out at a restaurant where I consulted. They were hemorrhaging new hires. Great candidates would show up excited on Day One and ghost them by Day Five. When I dug into it, here's what I found: New servers were handed a uniform, shown where the POS system was, shadowed someone for half a shift, then thrown on the floor during a Friday dinner rush. No real training. No context. No support system. Just "good luck." They weren't quitting because they couldn't do the job. They were quitting because they felt set up to fail.

Your job doesn't end when someone accepts your offer. That's when the real work begins.

Structured Onboarding Processes: The Framework That Actually Works

Let's be honest... most hospitality onboarding is a hot mess. It's a hodgepodge of "here's where we keep the linens" and "just watch what Maria does" with maybe a binder full of policies nobody reads. Then we act surprised when new hires either flounder or leave.

Real onboarding is a structured journey, not a scavenger hunt.

Here's what a real onboarding process looks like:

Pre-Day One (Yes, Onboarding Starts Before They Start): Send a welcome email or text a few days before they start. Include:

- What time to arrive and where to go
- What to bring (ID, banking info for direct deposit, etc.)
- What to wear
- Who they'll be meeting with
- A little excitement about having them join the team

This seems basic, but I can't tell you how many new hires show up anxious and confused because nobody told them what to expect. First impressions go both ways.

Day One... The Make-or-Break Day:

Do NOT waste Day One on paperwork. I know, I know... the I-9 forms need to get done. But if you spend their first three hours in a back office filling out tax forms, you've already lost them. Do the administrative stuff, but make it quick, and then get it connected to your operation and your people.

Your Day One should include:

- **A real welcome.** Introduce them to the team. Make them feel like people were expecting them and are happy they're here.
- **A property tour with context.** Don't just show them where things are. Explain WHY things are the way they are. "We keep extra linens here because we learned during a sold-out weekend that..." Stories create understanding.
- **Meeting key people across departments.** Even if they're a front desk agent, introduce them to housekeeping, maintenance, and F&B. In hospitality, everyone affects everyone.
- **Explaining the 'why' behind your operation.** What's your brand promise? What do guests expect? What makes you different? What are you trying to build?
- **A meal together.** Break bread with your new hire. This is hospitality. Human connection matters.

By the end of Day One, they should feel welcomed, not overwhelmed. They should understand the culture, not just the checklist.

Week One... Building the Foundation:

Week One is about structured learning, not trial by fire. I don't care how short staffed you are... resist the urge to throw them into full duty immediately. That short-term relief creates long-term problems.

Create a **structured training schedule** that includes:

- **Shadowing multiple people** in the role (not just one person, because everyone has different strengths and bad habits)
- **Hands on practice during slower periods**
- **Daily check ins** with a manager or trainer to answer questions and address concerns

- **Gradual responsibility increases**... on Day Three they observe, on Day Four they do tasks with oversight, by Day Seven they're handling responsibilities with backup nearby

Document this schedule. Write it down. Give them a copy. When people know what's coming, anxiety decreases and learning increases.

Weeks Two Through Four... Building Confidence:

This is where most onboarding falls apart. We assume they've "got it" and we disappear. But they're still figuring out the unwritten rules, the team dynamics, the guest patterns.

During this phase:

- **Assign increasingly complex tasks** but with a clear feedback loop
- **Have weekly structured check-ins** (not just "how's it going?" conversations)
- **Introduce them to different shifts and scenarios** so they understand the full rhythm of your operation
- **Let them make small mistakes** in controlled environments so they learn problem solving

For restaurants, this means working different day parts. For hotels, this means seeing different occupancy levels and guest types.

Months Two and Three... The Critical Window:

Here's where you're watching for two things: **competence and cultural fit.** They should be independently handling their responsibilities by now, but you should still be checking in regularly.

This is also when the honeymoon period ends and reality sets in. Are they still engaged? Are they integrating with the team? Are they meeting your standards?

Monthly structured reviews during this period are essential. More on that in a minute.

Setting Clear Expectations from Day One

Want to know the number one reason hospitality employees say they left a job? **Unclear expectations.**

They thought the job was one thing. It turned out to be something else. Nobody told them what success looked like. They got in trouble because things they didn't know were problems.

Clarity is kindness. Ambiguity is cruelty.

On Day One, sit down with your new hire and explicitly discuss:

Performance Standards:

- What does "great" look like in this role?
- What are the non-negotiables?
- How will they be evaluated?
- What are the most common mistakes people make in this position?

For a server: "Great means your section is turned efficiently, guests feel taken care of, you're supporting your team during the rush, and you're consistently hitting X guest satisfaction scores. A non-negotiable is following food safety protocols. We'll evaluate you on guest feedback, sales performance, and teamwork. The most common mistake new servers make is trying to do everything alone instead of asking for help."

See the difference between that and "just do a good job"?

Schedule and Availability Expectations: Be crystal clear about scheduling. How far in advance? How flexible do they need to be? What happens if they need time off? What's the policy on shift swaps?

I've seen new hires quit because they thought they had weekends off and then got scheduled for three straight Saturday nights. That's a failure of communication, not commitment.

Cultural and Behavioral Expectations: What's acceptable and what's not at your property? How do you handle conflict? What's your phone policy? How do you expect people to communicate? What are the unwritten rules that will get them in trouble if they break them?

Every operation has these. Make them written rules.

Growth and Development Path: Where can this job lead? What skills will they develop? When will they be eligible for raises or promotions? What do they need to do to advance?

Even if someone is taking a "just a job" position, knowing there's a path forward increases engagement.

Assigning Mentors or Buddies: The Secret Weapon

Here's what I know for sure: **new hires who have a buddy are 50% more likely to still be with you after six months.** I've seen this pattern at dozens of properties.

But here's what most places get wrong... they assign a buddy and then never follow up. The buddy system works when it's structured and supported.

How to make mentorship work:

Choose the right mentors. Don't just pick your top performer. Pick someone who is:

- Competent AND patient
- Respected by the team
- Good at explaining things
- Willing to do this (don't voluntell people)
- Representative of the culture you're trying to build

I'd rather have a solid B+ employee who's a natural teacher than an A+ employee who gets frustrated explaining things.

Give mentors real guidance. Don't just say "show them the ropes." Give them a checklist of what needs to be covered and when. Empower them to answer questions. Give them slightly reduced workloads during the first week so they have time to train.

Create natural connection points. The mentor should:

- Shadow the new hire during their first full shifts
- Have scheduled coffee or meal breaks together during Week One
- Be the person the new hire texts when they have questions
- Check in at the end of each shift during Week One
- Be available for questions during Weeks Two through Four

Recognize and reward mentors. If mentorship is important to your culture, it should be reflected in how you recognize people. Maybe mentors get a small bonus when their mentee successfully completes 90 days. Maybe it's part of advancement criteria. Maybe it's public recognition.

A luxury hotel group I worked with created a "Mentor of the Quarter" award. It became one of the most prestigious recognitions in the company. People WANTED to be mentors because it meant something.

The buddy system also helps with the invisible stuff. Where do people take breaks? Which manager should you go to with which type of problem? What do people do after work? Who are the people to learn from and who are the people to avoid? New hires need this social map, and a buddy provides it.

The Critical First 90 Days: What to Watch and When to Worry

The first 90 days tell you almost everything you need to know about whether someone will succeed long term. But you must pay attention.

Here's what you're watching for at each stage:

Days 1 to 14... The Enthusiasm Test: Are they showing up on time? Are they asking questions? Are they engaged during training? Do they seem excited or just going through the motions?

Red flags this early:

- Repeated lateness
- Disengagement during training
- Complaints about aspects of the job they knew about before accepting
- Not taking notes or asking clarifying questions
- Poor treatment of team members or guests during shadowing

If you're seeing these in Week One, you have a problem. Address it immediately. Don't hope it gets better.

Days 15 to 30... The Competence Check: Are they retaining what they learned? Can they execute basic tasks without constant supervision? Are they problem solving or constantly asking for help with things they should know by now?

Most important: **Are they coachable?** When you give feedback, do they implement it or get defensive? This is when you'll know if they have the aptitude for the role.

Days 31 to 60... The Cultural Fit Assessment: How are they integrating with the team? Are they supporting others? Do they align with your values during pressure moments? Are guests responding positively to them?

You're not looking for perfection. You're looking for trajectory. Are they getting better each week?

Days 61 to 90... The Independence Test: Can they handle full shifts without backup? Do they make good decisions? Have they moved from "learning" to "performing"?

By Day 90, you should have clarity. Either this person is going to be successful, or they're not.

Structured check-ins are non-negotiable during this period:

- **Day 3:** How's it going? Any questions about what you've learned so far?
- **End of Week 1:** What surprised you? What's been hardest? What do you need more help with?
- **End of Week 2:** Let's talk about what you're doing well and what we need to focus on developing.
- **Day 30 Review:** Formal sit down. Here's where you are. Here's where you need to be. Here's the plan to close the gap.

- **Day 60 Review:** Are we on track? Let's discuss what's working and what needs to adjust.
- **Day 90 Review:** You're now a full member of this team. Here's your performance assessment. Here's what comes next.

Document these conversations. Both for clarity and for legal protection if it doesn't work out.

How to Assess Whether Someone Is Succeeding in the Role

Assessment isn't just about catching problems. It's about reinforcing good behavior and course correcting early.

You need multiple data points:

Direct observation. Watch them work. Don't just rely on reports. See how they interact with guests, handle pressure, work with the team.

Guest feedback. What are guests saying? Are they getting mentioned positively? Are there complaints? In our digital world, guests tell you who's good.

Peer input. What does the team say? Are people happy to work with this person or do they groan when they see them on the schedule?

Operational metrics. For servers: table turn times, average check, guest satisfaction scores. For front desk: check in speed, upsell conversion, complaint resolution. Every role has measurable outputs.

The vibe check. How do they show up? Are they positive or negative? Do they bring energy or drain it? Do they take ownership or make excuses?

All these together give you a complete picture.

When you spot issues, address them immediately.
Don't wait until a review. "Hey, I noticed you've been late three times this week. What's going on?" Early intervention prevents bigger problems.

When you spot wins, celebrate them immediately.
"You absolutely crushed that difficult guest situation yesterday. That's exactly what great service looks like here." Positive reinforcement shapes behavior.

The Bottom Line on Onboarding

You can't hire well and onboard poorly and expect good outcomes.

The person you worked so hard to find, interview, and select deserves a structured path to success. They deserve clarity. They deserve support. They deserve to know whether they're winning or losing. Give them that, and most will rise to the occasion. Skimp on it, and you'll be hiring again in 60 days.

Your new hire's success isn't just their responsibility. It's yours. Set them up right, and they'll make you look brilliant. Forget about them after Day One, and they'll forget about you by Day Thirty.

The choice is yours.

Fostering a Culture of Teamwork and Excellence

Creating a Culture of Trust and Continuous Growth

Hospitality is an industry where feedback is constant, from guest reviews to daily operational evaluations. This culture of evaluation can, unfortunately, make managers apprehensive, constantly fearing their one misstep away from failure. This is where imposter syndrome takes a toll:

managers may start to dread evaluations, viewing them as a reflection of personal inadequacy rather than an opportunity for growth. And when managers fear feedback, they pass that fear onto their teams, creating an environment where both leaders and employees feel unsteady.

In my journey, I've learned that building resilience against imposter syndrome requires a shift in perspective. Feedback, both positive and constructive, is a tool for improvement, not a measure of worth. Just as a coach reviews each player's performance to identify areas of growth, managers can learn to view feedback as guidance rather than judgment. Over time, this mindset can transform evaluations from something intimidating into something empowering, allowing managers to embrace feedback as part of a continuous journey toward growth.

Think about Coach Scott standing on that field in Saudi Arabia. After every game, he'd gather us to review what happened. He'd point out mistakes, sure. But he never made those mistakes, which meant we were failures. He made them mean we had opportunities to get better.

"You left the near post exposed on that corner kick. Let's work on your positioning this week. "Not: "You're a terrible goalkeeper." The difference is everything.

Through experience, I've found that developing a growth-oriented culture means setting up clear frameworks for feedback. Leaders must establish early on that feedback is not personal but purposeful, serving to refine skills and foster team cohesion. I advocate for structured check-ins, scheduled consistently and framed constructively, as these regular sessions build trust between manager and team members.

A 90-day feedback session, for example, can become a checkpoint to evaluate alignment with the role and clarify expectations, ensuring both parties feel engaged and empowered. Regular feedback should never be a surprise.

When you establish a rhythm of ongoing conversations about performance, development, and goals, feedback becomes normal rather than threatening. It's just how we operate. It's how we all get better together.

Building the Foundation

Here's how to create a culture where feedback drives growth rather than fear:

Normalize Feedback as Part of Daily Operations

Don't save feedback for formal reviews. Make it a regular part of how you work together. After a busy shift, take five minutes to highlight what went well and identify one thing to improve next time. After a challenging guest interaction, debrief immediately while the experience is fresh. When feedback is constant and most positive, occasional constructive feedback doesn't feel like an attack; it feels like helpful coaching.

Model Receptiveness to Feedback

If you want your team to be open to feedback, you must model that openness yourself. Ask your team for feedback on your leadership. "What could I do differently to support you better?" "What's one thing I should stop doing?" "How can I improve our team meetings?" When you receive feedback, listen without defensiveness. Thank the person for their honesty. If appropriate, act on what you hear. When your team sees you accepting and implementing feedback, they'll be far more willing to do the same.

Separate Performance from Worth

Make it crystal clear that performance feedback is about behavior and results, not about someone's value as a person. A server who forgets to greet tables promptly needs to improve their greeting protocol.

That doesn't mean they're a bad person or a failure. It means they have a specific skill to develop. This distinction seems obvious, but in practice, many managers blur the line.

They let frustration with performance become frustration with the person. Don't do that. Keep feedback behavioral and specific.

Celebrating Growth and Effort

When someone implements feedback and improves, they acknowledge it publicly. "I want to recognize Marcus for the work he's put into his time management. Three weeks ago, we talked about strategies for staying organized during busy shifts, and I've seen real improvement.

Great job. This serves multiple purposes: it reinforces positive behavior, shows that you notice improvement, and demonstrates to the entire team that feedback leads to growth and recognition.

Industry Insight: Coach Eberbach on Culture-Building

Coach Eberbach's "Head, Heart, and Hands" philosophy provides a powerful framework for building a culture of teamwork and excellence in hospitality.

Head: The Strategic Mindset. "Every team needs to understand not only what they're doing but why they're doing it," he explained. He begins each season by setting concrete goals with his players, ensuring that every team member understands the overall mission. When players know their purpose, it translates into a stronger drive on the field. They're not just following instructions; they're motivated by a deeper understanding of the 'why.'

In hospitality, this means ensuring every team member understands how their role contributes to the guest experience and the operation's success. It's not just "clean the room." It's "create a sanctuary where weary travelers feel cared for."

Heart: The Emotional Connection. "To lead a team effectively, you need to connect with them on an emotional level," Coach Eberbach emphasized. He makes it a point to know his players personally: their strengths, challenges, and aspirations.

"Every player brings their own story to the field. When you acknowledge that, you can motivate them in ways that resonate deeply."

By fostering an environment of mutual respect and open communication, Coach Eberbach cultivates loyalty and dedication within his team, encouraging players to support one another and work toward shared goals. When team members feel genuinely cared for as individuals, they invest more deeply in the team's success.

Hands: Physical Action. "At the end of the day, you have to put in the work," Coach Eberbach stated. His practices are intense and demanding, designed to build not only the physical skills required for the game but also discipline and resilience. "When you're out on the field, you don't have time to think about the mechanics. It needs to be instinctive, and that only comes from hours of dedicated practice."

In hospitality, this translates to thorough training, consistent practice of service standards, and the discipline to execute excellently even under pressure. Excellence is not accidental; it's the result of deliberate, repeated practice. By integrating Head, Heart, and Hands into your hospitality operation, you create a culture where team members understand their purpose, feel emotionally connected to the mission and each other, and have the skills and discipline to execute at the highest level.

Monitoring Performance and Providing Constructive Feedback

The Peanut Butter and Jelly Approach to Evaluations

One of the simplest yet most effective analogies I've found for conducting evaluations is the "peanut butter and jelly" approach. This analogy has been instrumental in making feedback sessions more approachable, transforming what might otherwise be daunting or uncomfortable into something familiar and digestible.

When I coach managers on giving feedback, I introduce the idea of "sandwiching" constructive feedback with positive reinforcement. By beginning with the positives, transitioning to constructive points in the middle, and closing with further strengths, we build evaluations that are balanced, supportive, and specific.

Just like making a peanut butter and jelly sandwich, each layer has a purpose, and each serves to create a whole that's greater than the sum of its parts. Through this approach, managers can deliver evaluations with clarity and compassion, ensuring their feedback is heard without overshadowing the employee's accomplishments.

Let me break down how this works in practice:

The First Slice: Start with Genuine Recognition

Begin the conversation by acknowledging what the employee does well. This isn't about false flattery or manipulation; it's about genuinely recognizing their strengths and contributions.

"Sarah, I want to start by saying how much I appreciate your dedication to guest satisfaction. You consistently go above and beyond to make guests feel welcome, and I've received multiple positive comments about your warm, professional demeanor." This opening serves several purposes. First, it puts the employee at ease. Second, it demonstrates that you notice and value their positive contributions. Third, it creates a foundation of trust and goodwill that makes the constructive feedback easier to hear. The key is authenticity. Don't manufacture compliments. Find genuine strengths to acknowledge. Every employee has them.

The Filling: Address Areas for Growth

Once you've established the positive context, transition to the areas that need improvement. Be specific, focus on observable behaviors, and offer concrete suggestions for development.

"There's one area where I think you have an opportunity to grow. I've noticed that during busy periods, your response time to guest requests sometimes slows down.

For example, last Friday during the evening rush, table seven waited nearly fifteen minutes for water refills, and table twelve's dessert order was delayed. I know you care about service quality, so I want to work with you on strategies for managing high-volume periods more effectively."

Notice what this does. It's specific (actual examples, not vague generalizations). It focuses on behavior (response time, specific incidents) not character. It frames the issue as an opportunity for growth. It expresses confidence in the employee's abilities and intentions. It offers partnership in finding solutions.

This is constructive feedback that helps someone improve, rather than just making them feel bad.

The Second Slice: Close with Encouragement and Next Steps

End the conversation by returning to the positive, reiterating your confidence in the employee, and establishing clear next steps.

"Sarah, I have complete confidence in your ability to manage this. Your natural warmth and commitment to guests are exactly what we need. Let's work together on some time management strategies for busy shifts. I'd like to meet with you again in two weeks to check in on your progress. I'm here to support you, and I'm excited to see you continue to grow in this role."

This closing accomplishes several things. It reminds the employees of their value. It provides clear next steps. It establishes accountability through follow-up. It offers support rather than leaving them to figure it out alone. It expresses optimism about their future success.

Why This Approach Works

The peanut butter and jelly method works because it creates psychological safety. When employees know that their strengths are recognized, they're far more open to hearing about areas where they can improve. The positive context doesn't dilute the constructive feedback; it makes it more likely to be heard and acted upon.

I've seen managers try to deliver feedback without this framework, jumping straight to criticism. The employee becomes defensive, shuts down, and nothing improves. The feedback, however accurate, becomes wasted because it never penetrates the wall of defensiveness. The sandwich approach dismantles that wall. It says: "I see you. I value you. I believe in you. And I'm going to help you get better." That's a message people can hear and act on.

Addressing Underperformance: The Performance Improvement Plan

Sometimes, despite regular feedback and support, an employee continues to underperform. This is one of the most challenging aspects of leadership in hospitality. It requires difficult conversations, clear documentation, and a structured approach to helping the employee either improve or transition out of the role. A Performance Improvement Plan (PIP) is a formal tool for addressing persistent performance issues. Done well, a PIP provides the employee with a clear roadmap for improvement, specific expectations, measurable goals, and defined timeframes. Done poorly, it becomes a bureaucratic exercise that everyone knows is just the prelude to termination.

The difference lies in your approach and intention.

The Coach's Perspective on PIPs

From a coaching standpoint, a PIP should be viewed as a development opportunity, not a punishment. Just as a coach might create a specialized training program for a player struggling with a particular skill, managers should approach PIPs as structured support systems designed to help employees succeed. The goal of a PIP is not merely to document failure; it's to create the conditions for success. Think about it this way: if you genuinely believe the employee can improve and you're committed to helping them do so, the PIP becomes a tool for development. If you've already decided the employee needs to go and you're just checking boxes to protect yourself legally, the employee will sense that, and the PIP becomes a charade.

Be honest with yourself about your intentions. If the employee truly cannot succeed in the role and you know it, have the courage to make that decision cleanly rather than putting them through a drawn-out process that offers false hope. If you genuinely believe improvement is possible, commit fully to making it happen.

Creating an Effective PIP

Identify Specific Performance Issues

Be crystal clear about what's not working. Vague statements like "poor attitude" or "not meeting expectations" aren't helpful. What specific behaviors or results are problematic? "Over the past two months, you've been late to your shift seven times, averaging fifteen minutes late. On three occasions, you failed to complete your closing checklist, leaving tasks undone for the opening shift. Guest satisfaction scores for your service have averaged 3.2 out of 5, below our standard of 4.0."

This specificity serves two purposes: it makes the problem undeniable, and it makes improvement measurable. You'll know if the employee is succeeding because you can count late arrivals, review checklists, and track satisfaction scores.

Set Clear, Measurable Goals

Based on performance issues, establish specific goals that define success. These should be SMART: Specific, Measurable, Achievable, Relevant, and Time-bound.

"Over the next 60 days, you will: Arrive on time for all scheduled shifts (no more than one late arrival excused for emergency). Complete 100% of closing checklist items before leaving each shift.

Achieve an average guest satisfaction score of 4.0 or higher. Complete customer service training module by day 30." These goals leave no ambiguity. Both you and the employee will know exactly whether they're meeting expectations.

Provide Resources and Support

A PIP should include support, not just demands. What training, mentoring, or resources will you provide to help the employee improve? "To support your success, we will: Enroll you in our advanced customer service training program. Pair you with Marcus, one of our top performing servers, for mentorship.

Conduct weekly check-ins to review progress and address challenges. Provide a revised closing checklist with clearer procedures."

This demonstrates your commitment to the employees' success and gives them the tools they need to improve.

Establish Regular Check-Ins

Don't wait until the end of the PIP period to evaluate progress. Schedule regular check-ins (weekly or bi-weekly) to review what's working, what's not, and what adjustments might be needed.

These check-ins serve multiple purposes. They provide ongoing feedback rather than saving everything for the end. They allow course correction if something isn't working. They demonstrate your active engagement in the employees' development. They create documentation of the process.

Document Everything

Keep detailed records of the PIP process, including the original plan, check-in conversations, specific incidents (positive and negative), and the employee's progress toward goals.

This documentation serves two purposes: it protects the organization if termination becomes necessary, and it provides a clear record of improvement if the employee succeeds.

Conclude with Clarity

At the end of the PIP period, the outcome should be clear. Either the employee has met the goals and continues in the role (perhaps with ongoing monitoring), or they have not met the goals and employment is terminated.

Don't let ambiguity cloud this decision. If someone has genuinely improved, they acknowledge that success and provide a path forward. If they haven't, honor the process by following through with the consequences.

The Goal: Development, Not Documentation

The goal of a structured approach to addressing underperformance is not merely to correct behavior but to help the employee succeed and thrive.

A coach's goal is not only to make a player fit the team's current strategy but to develop their full potential, enabling them to contribute meaningfully and grow as an individual.

In the workplace, the PIP is more than a checklist; it's a tool for development, motivation, and personal achievement. By setting clear goals, providing training and mentorship, reviewing progress regularly, and fostering open communication, managers create a pathway for employees to rediscover their strengths and realize their potential.

By implementing this structured approach, managers not only help the individual employee improve but also reinforce a culture of accountability, support, and continuous development within the organization.

Conflict Resolution: The Coach's Approach

Addressing conflicts within a team is much like a coach handling dispute among players on the field; a clear, structured approach is essential for maintaining harmony, focus, and trust.

From a coach's perspective, conflicts are inevitable in any high-performance setting where individuals with different perspectives, skills, and personalities work closely together under pressure. The key to successful conflict resolution is not to ignore or downplay issues but to address them constructively and promptly, creating a safe environment where everyone feels heard and respected.

Building a Foundation of Respect

The first step in effective conflict resolution is fostering a culture of respect and collaboration from the outset. A coach knows that a strong, unified team doesn't happen by chance; it requires consistent effort in building relationships and setting expectations.

In the workplace, creating this culture means that managers should emphasize the importance of teamwork, respect, and mutual support in daily interactions, training sessions, and team meetings. This proactive approach sets a foundation where employees understand that differences will be addressed respectfully and collaboratively, rather than through blame or avoidance.

When respect is built into the culture from day one, conflicts are less likely to escalate into personal attacks or deep divisions. People disagree about methods and approaches, but they maintain respect for each other as professionals.

Address Conflicts Promptly

When conflicts do arise, it's essential for managers to address them promptly. Just as a coach wouldn't let a player's disagreement with a teammate fester and affect their game, managers should step in as soon as they become aware of tension within the team.

Addressing conflicts early prevents them from escalating into more significant issues that can disrupt team dynamics and impact performance.

I learned this lesson the hard way early in my management career. I noticed tension between two front-desk agents but convinced myself it would blow over. It didn't. It festered. Other team members chose sides. The entire department became toxic. By the time I finally intervened, the damage was significant and took months to repair.

Now, I address conflicts immediately. Not aggressively or heavy-handedly, but promptly and directly.

Creating a Safe Space for Dialogue

Creating a safe space for conflict resolution is crucial, as it allows team members to express their concerns openly without fear of retaliation or judgment.

In sports, a coach may hold private meetings with players to discuss any grievances, providing a neutral, supportive space for resolving issues. Similarly, in the workplace, managers can establish private, respectful settings for conflict resolution, where employees feel comfortable sharing their feelings and perspectives.

By creating a safe, structured environment for these conversations, managers help employees address issues directly and respectfully, reducing the likelihood of lingering resentment or unresolved conflicts that could impact team morale.

Key Elements of Safe Space: Privacy (not in front of other team members). Neutrality (the manager as facilitator, not judge). Ground rules (no interruptions, no personal attacks, focus on issues not personalities). Active listening (both parties must truly hear each other). Confidentiality (what's discussed stays between those involved).

Structured Mediation Process

A structured mediation process can be invaluable in resolving conflicts constructively. Just as a coach would facilitate a discussion between two players who disagree on game strategy, guiding them towards a shared understanding, managers should act as neutral facilitators, helping employees explore solutions together.

The Mediation Framework:

Step 1: Set the Stage. Begin by establishing ground rules and explaining the process. Make it clear that the goal is resolution, not blame. Both parties will have a chance to speak without interruption.

Step 2: Each Party Shares Their Perspective. Allow each person to explain their view of the situation without interruption. The manager takes notes and asks clarifying questions but doesn't judge or take sides.

Step 3: Identify the Core Issue. Often, conflict that's visible isn't the real problem. Two servers might be arguing about who takes which tables, but the real issue is that one feels the other gets preferential treatment from management.

Dig deeper to find the root cause.

Step 4: Brainstorm Solutions Together. Ask both parties what they think would help resolve the situation. Encourage creative problem-solving. Often, employees can find solutions the manager wouldn't have considered.

Step 5: Agree on a Path Forward. Establish specific actions each person will take, timeframes for implementation, and a follow-up date to ensure the resolution is working.

Step 6: Document and Follow Up. Write down the agreement and give copies to both parties. Schedule a follow-up meeting to assess how the resolution works and adjusts if needed.

Encourage Open Communication

Encouraging open communication is another critical component of effective conflict resolution. A coach knows that players need to communicate freely with one another to build trust and synchronize their efforts on the field.

In the workplace, managers should promote open communication channels where employees feel comfortable discussing potential issues before they escalate into conflicts. Regular team meetings or one-on-one check-ins provide opportunities for employees to voice any concerns or frustrations in a supportive setting.

Lead with Empathy

Empathy is essential throughout the conflict resolution process, as it helps managers connect with employees on a personal level and understand their perspectives.

Just as a coach might approach a struggling player with empathy, seeking to understand the emotions behind their actions, managers should take the time to listen to each employee's feelings and experiences during a conflict.

By acknowledging each person's unique circumstances, managers demonstrate that they value their team members as individuals, not just as employees. This approach fosters a culture of compassion, where employees feel supported and are more likely to approach conflicts with understanding and patience.

Train Your Team in Conflict Resolution

Training in conflict resolution skills can also empower employees to handle disagreements independently, reducing the need for managerial intervention.

In sports, a coach might teach players strategies for resolving disputes among themselves, fostering a more self-sufficient team dynamic. Similarly, managers can provide training sessions or workshops focused on conflict resolution, helping employees build skills in active listening, empathy, and collaborative problem-solving.

By equipping employees with these skills, managers encourage a proactive approach to conflict resolution, where team members feel confident in addressing issues directly and respectfully with one another. This self-sufficiency strengthens the team's ability to maintain harmony and resilience, even in challenging situations.

The Foundation of Strong Leadership

In essence, establishing a clear process for resolving conflicts is essential for maintaining a positive, productive work environment. From a coach's perspective, addressing conflicts early, creating a safe space for dialogue, and fostering open communication all contribute to a cohesive, high-performing team.

Managers who approach conflict resolution with empathy, structure, and a commitment to collaboration build a foundation of trust and respect within the team, empowering employees to work through challenges constructively. This approach not only resolves immediate issues but also strengthens the team's resilience and unity, preparing them to navigate future conflicts with confidence and mutual support.

Leadership in hospitality is not about having all the answers or being perfect. It's about creating an environment where people can grow, where feedback flows freely, where conflicts get resolved constructively, and where everyone feels valued and supported. When you combine authentic leadership with structured processes for feedback, performance management, and conflict resolution, you create a culture where both individuals and the organization can thrive.

That's the goal. That's the work. That's what separates good hospitality operations from truly great ones. Lead with authenticity. Provide clear feedback. Address issues promptly. Resolve conflicts with empathy. And watch your team transform from a collection of individuals into a unified force capable of delivering exceptional hospitality experiences. Just like Coach Scott taught me on those dusty fields in Saudi Arabia: it's not about being perfect. It's about showing up, being real, and helping everyone around you get better every single day.

That's coaching. That's leadership. That's how you build something that lasts.

Learning How to Win Even Through Loss: Winning Through Mistakes

Coach Scott and Coach Eberbach have spent years building teams that know how to persevere, even when facing defeat. They both understand that success isn't just about winning; it's about learning from losses and turning setbacks into steppingstones for future victories. For these coaches, every failure presents an opportunity for growth and improvement, whether on the soccer field or in the hospitality industry. Learning how to win through a loss is an essential skill they teach their players and team members alike, framing each challenge as a building block toward resilience and mastery.

Embracing Failures as Learning Opportunities

For Coach Scott, the philosophy of embracing failure as a learning opportunity is foundational to his coaching approach. He recalls the early days of his coaching career, where he quickly learned that a team's reaction to loss often had a greater impact on their future success than any single victory. "Every loss gives us something valuable," he would say. "We just have to be willing to look for the lesson."

In his view, losses aren't failures; they're moments for reflection and analysis. After each disappointing game, Coach Scott holds team meetings to dissect what went wrong. This isn't about placing blame or criticizing individual performances. Instead, he uses these sessions as an opportunity to build his players' understanding of strategy and team dynamics. "I want each player to see where we could have done better as a team, not as individuals. When everyone understands their role in the loss, they're more prepared to contribute to future wins."

Coach Eberbach takes a similar approach, but he adds an additional layer of resilience-building into his response to failures. For him, the idea is not just to analyze losses but to cultivate a mindset that sees setbacks as temporary. He encourages his players to see each loss as one more step in their journey toward success, reminding them that failures are a normal part of growth. "In sports, and in life, we're going to face losses," he says. "But if you approach every game as a learning opportunity, you'll find that even the toughest defeats can prepare you for the future."

After a tough loss, he has his players focus on what went well, even if the final score doesn't reflect it. This exercise helps his team stay positive and maintain perspective, reinforcing the idea that growth is a continuous process.

Both coaches recognize that this approach is just as relevant in hospitality. When a hotel experiences a decline in guest satisfaction, it can feel like a blow to the entire team. Coach Scott sees parallels between his team's post-game analysis sessions and a hotel's approach to handling negative feedback. "Just like we watch game footage to see what went wrong, a hotel should examine guest feedback and find areas for improvement," he says.

He encourages hospitality managers to take a systematic approach, treating each complaint as a chance to improve service. "A complaint is really a customer saying, 'Here's what you could do better,'" he explains. "It's a gift, not a setback." By approaching complaints with this mindset, Coach Scott believes that hospitality teams can turn negative feedback into a roadmap for growth.

Turning Setbacks into Strategy

Coach Eberbach emphasizes that every setback has the potential to provide a more effective strategy for the future. He recounts a particularly difficult season where his team suffered consecutive losses and morale was at an all-time low. Rather than dwelling on the losses, he saw an opportunity to rethink the team's strategy. "I asked myself, what were we missing? What needed to change?" he recalls.

He began experimenting with different formations, adjusting his approach based on the specific skills and strengths of his players. Over time, the team adapted and became stronger, eventually ending the season on a high note.

"Sometimes, you have to shake things up," he says. "If you keep doing the same thing and getting the same result, it's time to try something new."

Coach Scott also believes that adaptability is key to winning through loss. After a loss, he leads his team through a reflective process where they discuss what worked, what didn't, and how they can adjust their tactics for the next game. "In soccer, like in business, you can't control everything," he explains. "But you can control how you respond and adjust."

He often tells his players that flexibility is one of the most valuable traits in any successful team, as it allows them to adapt quickly to changes and challenges. This principle is equally important in hospitality. Coach Scott encourages hotel managers to be willing to pivot when they see areas that need improvement. Whether it's changing a process or adjusting the way employees interact with guests, he believes that flexibility and responsiveness can turn a setback into an opportunity.

For Coach Eberbach, turning setbacks into strategy involves not only looking at what went wrong but also taking time to recognize what went right. In the face of a disappointing season, he reviews not only the losses but also the successes and near-wins. "We need to understand both our strengths and weaknesses," he says. "When we can look at our performance holistically, we're better prepared to tackle challenges moving forward."

This balanced approach to reflection ensures that his players see a loss as part of a larger journey rather than a failure. In hospitality, he advises leaders to take a similar approach: to analyze every piece of feedback, both positive and negative, and find patterns that can guide future decisions.

Cultivating a Resilient Mindset

Building resilience in his players is one of Coach Scott's core values. He believes that resilience isn't just about getting back up after a fall but about learning to weather challenges without losing focus or enthusiasm. "The teams that succeed are the ones that can keep their heads up, even when things aren't going their way," he says.

To him, resilience is as much a skill as any technical ability, and he builds it through challenging practices that test his players' endurance, focus, and determination. After a tough game, he uses resilience exercises to help his players regain confidence and prepare for the next match. "We talk about what we learned, how we can improve, and what we're proud of from that game," he explains. By acknowledging both the successes and the setbacks, he helps his players build a balanced, resilient mindset.

Coach Eberbach's approach to resilience is similar but has a distinct focus on mental toughness. He believes that mental resilience is often what separates great players from good ones. "When we're facing a tough opponent or coming back from a loss, it's not just about skill; it's about mental strength," he says.

He incorporates exercises into his training that challenge his players' ability to stay focused under pressure. For example, he might have complete drills while being timed or create situations that mimic high-stress game scenarios. This teaches his players to stay calm and composed, even when the stakes are high. Coach Eberbach believes that this kind of resilience is critical in the hospitality industry as well, where the ability to remain calm under pressure can make all the difference in guest interactions. In hospitality, both coaches see resilience as an essential skill for team members who must often face high-stress situations and challenge guests. Coach Scott recommends that hospitality leaders create an environment where employees feel supported and can learn from difficult interactions without fear of reprimand. "If you create a safe space where employees can learn from mistakes, you'll build a more resilient team," he says.

Coach Eberbach agrees, adding that a resilient mindset in hospitality can turn a potentially negative guest experience into an opportunity to showcase exceptional service. He encourages managers to train employees to remain composed and positive, no matter the situation, as this mindset can often turn a setback into a memorable guest experience.

Accountability as a Tool for Growth

For both Coach Scott and Coach Eberbach, accountability is the bedrock of growth and improvement. When things don't go as planned, the first step they take is to encourage their players to own up to their part in the outcome. Coach Scott sees this to foster maturity and a sense of responsibility within his team. "I tell my players, 'We're all in this together. If we lose, it's on all of us, and if we win, it's because we all did our part.'"

This philosophy of shared accountability strengthens team bonds and creates a culture where everyone is committed to their roles. Coach Scott believes that, over time, this approach makes each player more mindful of their actions and their impact on the team. Coach Eberbach's method of instilling accountability is similar, but he also emphasizes the importance of self-reflection. After each game, he asks his players to identify one thing they did well and one area where they could improve. "It's about taking ownership of your growth," he says.

By reflecting on their performance, players develop a deeper understanding of their strengths and weaknesses, which allows them to make targeted improvements. In the hospitality industry, he encourages managers to use a similar process. "If every team member can reflect on their day and ask, 'What did I do well, and what could I have done better?' the whole team will grow," he explains. This practice of reflection and accountability builds a culture of continuous improvement, where everyone is responsible for both their successes and their failures.

Transforming Failures into Opportunities

One of the most valuable lessons that both coaches instill in their teams is the ability to turn failures into opportunities. For Coach Scott, this means embracing a mindset of possibility and looking for ways to reframe setbacks. He recalls a season when his team failed to advance in a major tournament. Instead of focusing on the disappointment, he gathered his players and challenged them to set new goals for the following season. "We asked ourselves, 'What can we do differently next time?'" he says.

The team came back the next year with a renewed sense of purpose and won the championship. "Sometimes, a setback is just what you need to push yourself to the next level," he says. This mindset shift allows players to see failures as temporary and as steppingstones toward greater accomplishments.

Coach Eberbach teaches his players to view setbacks as opportunities for self-discovery. He believes that challenges reveal character, showing players who they are when faced with adversity. In hospitality, he advises managers to adopt this mindset and encourage their teams to do the same. A drop in guest satisfaction scores, for example, might be seen as a chance to reassess and improve service standards. "Instead of seeing it as a failure, see it as a call to action," he advises. By approaching setbacks as opportunities to grow and innovate, Coach Eberbach believes that hospitality teams can develop a proactive culture that values continuous improvement.

Final Reflections: Redefining Success

For Coach Scott and Coach Eberbach, winning through a loss ultimately redefines the concept of success. In their view, true success isn't measured solely by victories or accolades but by a team's ability to grow, adapt, and stay resilient in the face of challenges. They believe that a team's response to failure is a greater indicator of success than the number of wins on the scoreboard. "Success isn't just about the end result; it's about the journey, the lessons learned, and the growth achieved along the way," Coach Scott says.

In both soccer and hospitality, setbacks are inevitable. Yet, with the guidance and perspectives of coaches like Scott and Eberbach, teams can learn how to turn losses into powerful motivators for growth. By embracing failure as a steppingstone, adapting strategies, fostering resilience, and holding themselves accountable, they create a foundation of success that transcends any single game or guest interaction. For these coaches, learning how to win through loss is the true mark of a champion, in sports, business, and life.

Applying This to Hospitality: Practical Steps

1. Conduct Post-Incident Reviews. Just as coaches review game footage, conduct brief debriefs after service challenges. Focus on learning, not blame.

2. Track Patterns, Not Just Incidents. One complaint is data. Ten similar complaints is a pattern that requires strategic adjustment.

3. Celebrate Recoveries. When a team member turns a negative situation into a positive guest experience, recognize it publicly. This reinforces that mistakes are opportunities.

4. Build Resilience Through Training. Create scenarios in training that simulate high-pressure situations, allowing staff to practice staying calm and solution focused.

5. Encourage Reflection. At the end of each shift or weekly team meeting, ask: "What did we learn this week? What will we do differently next time?"

6. Share Your Own Failures. As a leader, model vulnerability by sharing your own mistakes and what you learned from them. This creates psychological safety for others to do the same.

Failures should be viewed as learning opportunities rather than setbacks. Both soccer teams and hospitality businesses have faced failures and emerged stronger by learning from their mistakes. By remaining committed to excellence in hiring and management, managers can build high-performing teams that drive business success, teams that don't just survive challenges but use them as fuel for continuous improvement. The hardest losses often precede the greatest victories. The question is not whether your team will face setbacks; they will. The question is whether you'll create a culture where those setbacks become the foundation for future success.

Chapter Summary and Key Takeaways

Throughout this chapter, we've explored how coaching principles from the soccer field translate powerfully to hospitality leadership. The parallels are striking both environments demand high performance under pressure, require seamless teamwork, and depend on individuals who can be coached to excellence.

Key Principles to Remember:

1. **Authentic Leadership Builds Trust.** Your team doesn't need you to be perfect. They need you to be real, vulnerable, and committed to growth alongside them.
2. **Character Matters More Than Credentials.** Technical skills can be taught. Character traits (resilience, empathy, accountability) are either present or they're not.
3. **Recognize Un-Coachable Behaviors Early.** The eight un-coachable behaviors we've outlined are red flags that should guide your hiring decisions and performance management. Protecting your team

culture means having the courage to address these issues decisively.

4. **Feedback is a Gift, not a Punishment.** When you create a culture where feedback flows freely and constructively, your team becomes self-correcting and continuously improving.

5. **Conflict is Inevitable; Resolution is a Choice.** Address conflicts promptly and with structure. Unresolved tension poisons even the strongest teams.

6. **Learn from Every Loss.** Mistakes, setbacks, and failures are not the opposite of success; they're part of the path to it. How you respond to challenges defines your team's culture.

The journey to building a high-performing hospitality team requires both systematic processes and genuine human connection. You need structured interview guides and behavioral assessments, but you also need to trust your instincts about character. You need clear performance metrics and improvement plans, but you also need to lead with empathy and authenticity. Most importantly, you need to view yourself not just as a manager, but as a coach, someone committed to bringing out the best in every team member, creating an environment where excellence becomes the standard, and building something that lasts beyond any single shift, season, or success. As Coach Scott told me years ago on that dusty field in Saudi Arabia: "The game is never really about the game. It's about the people you become while playing it."

In hospitality, the work is never really about the rooms, the meals, or the reservations. It's about the people who deliver those experiences and the leader who helps them become their best selves in the process. That's the game worth playing. That's the victory worth pursuing. Now go out there and coach your team to greatness.

References

Ahmed, U., & Elsayed, M. (2022). The impact of hospitality work environment on employees' turnover intentions during COVID-19 pandemic: The mediating role of work-family conflict. *Frontiers in Psychology, 13,* 890418.

Al-Abri, M. H., Al Kouba, N., & Durrah, O. (2023). Hotel employees' burnout and intention to quit: The role of psychological distress and financial well-being in a moderation mediation model. *Behavioral Sciences, 13*(3), 215.

American Hotel & Lodging Association. (2023). *State of the hotel industry report.* Washington, DC: AHLA.

Bass, B. M. (1985). *Leadership and performance beyond expectations.* New York: Free Press.

Bernard, N. S., Dollinger, S. J., & Ramaniah, N. V. (2002). Applying the big five personality factors to the impostor phenomenon. *Journal of Personality Assessment, 78*(2), 321-333.

Borzillo, S. (2023). Leadership based on wellbeing. In *EHL Hospitality Insights.* Lausanne: EHL Group.

Boushey, H., & Glynn, S. J. (2012). There are significant business costs to replacing employees. *Center for American Progress, 16.*

Bransford, J. D., & Schwartz, D. L. (1999). Rethinking transfer: A simple proposal with multiple implications. *Review of Research in Education, 24,* 61-100.

Buick, I., & Thomas, M. (2001). Why do middle managers in hotels burn out? *International Journal of Contemporary Hospitality Management, 13*(6), 304-309.

Bureau of Labor Statistics. (2023). *Labor force statistics from the current population survey.* U.S. Department of Labor.

Burns, J. M. (1978). *Leadership.* New York: Harper & Row.

Cameron, K. S., & Quinn, R. E. (2011). *Diagnosing and changing organizational culture.* San Francisco: Jossey Bass.

Celayix. (2024). *Employee turnover in the hospitality industry.* Retrieved from https://www.celayix.com

Choi, Y., & Joung, H. W. (2017). Employee job satisfaction and customer oriented behavior: A study of frontline employees in the foodservice industry. *Journal of Human Resources in Hospitality & Tourism, 16*(3), 235-251.

Chrisman, S. M., Pieper, W. A., Clance, P. R., Holland, C. L., & Glickauf-Hughes, C. (1995). Validation of the Clance Imposter Phenomenon Scale. *Journal of Personality Assessment, 65*(3), 456-467.

Clance, P. R., & Imes, S. A. (1978). The imposter phenomenon in high achieving women. *Psychotherapy: Theory, Research & Practice, 15*(3), 241-247.

CultureMonkey. (2024). *Work-life balance in hospitality industry.* Retrieved from https://www.culturemonkey.io

Davidson, M. C., Timo, N., & Wang, Y. (2010). How much does labour turnover cost? *International Journal of Contemporary Hospitality Management, 22*(4), 451-466.

Dweck, C. S. (2006). *Mindset: The new psychology of success.* New York: Random House.

Edmondson, A. (1999). Psychological safety and learning behavior in work teams. *Administrative Science Quarterly, 44*(2), 350-383.

EHL Hospitality Insights. (2023). *Wellbeing first: A guide to managing burnout in the workplace.* Retrieved from https://hospitalityinsights.ehl.edu

Ellinger, A. D., Ellinger, A. E., & Keller, S. B. (2003). Supervisory coaching behavior, employee satisfaction, and warehouse employee performance. *Human Resource Development Quarterly, 14*(4), 435-458.

Fernandez-Vidal, J., Perks, S., & Orús, C. (2022). Digital transformation of the workforce in emerging economies. *Technological Forecasting and Social Change, 174,* 121257.

Forson, M. A., Hao, F., & Cheung, C. (2025). Women's career and imposter syndrome: Moderating effects of female role model and diversity management in the hospitality and tourism sector. *International Journal of Contemporary Hospitality Management, 37*(3), 1121-1144.

Giousmpasoglou, C., Marinakou, E., Papavasileiou, E., & Hall, K. (2025). *The imposter syndrome among chefs: A global survey.* Technical Report. Bournemouth University.

Goleman, D. (1995). *Emotional intelligence.* New York: Bantam Books.

Hamlin, R. G., Ellinger, A. D., & Beattie, R. S. (2006). Coaching at the heart of managerial effectiveness. *Human Resource Development International, 9*(3), 305-316.

Herzberg, F. (1959). *The motivation to work.* New York: John Wiley & Sons.

Huang, Y., Li, X., & Ma, E. (2019). The impact of work-family conflict on well-being in tourism and hospitality. *International Journal of Hospitality Management, 78,* 269-277.

Jung, H. S., & Yoon, H. H. (2015). The impact of employees' positive psychological capital on job satisfaction and organizational citizenship behaviors in the hotel. *International Journal of Contemporary Hospitality Management, 27*(6), 1135-1156.

Karatepe, O. M., & Aleshinloye, K. D. (2009). Emotional dissonance and emotional exhaustion among hotel employees in Nigeria. *International Journal of Hospitality Management, 28*(3), 349-358.

Kluger, A. N., & DeNisi, A. (1996). The effects of feedback interventions on performance. *Psychological Bulletin, 119*(2), 254-284.

Korn Ferry. (2024). *Leadership survey: Imposter syndrome among executives.* Korn Ferry Institute.

KPMG. (2020). *Women in leadership study.* KPMG International.

Kumawat, E., Datta, A., Prentice, C., & Leung, R. (2024). Artificial intelligence through the lens of hospitality employees. *International Journal of Hospitality Management, 123,* 103817.

Lee, J., Kim, J., & Oh, H. (2012). Managing customer orientation in tourism and hospitality. *Tourism Management, 33*(2), 429-437.

Lee, K. Y., & Way, K. (2010). Individual employment characteristics of hotel employees that play a role in employee satisfaction and work retention. *International Journal of Hospitality Management, 29*(3), 344-353.

Lee, S., Kim, M., & Park, S. (2025). Navigating artificial intelligence adoption in hospitality: Managerial insights and workforce transformation. *International Journal of Hospitality Management, 128,* 103912.

Liu, W., & Batt, R. (2010). How supervisors influence performance: A multilevel study of coaching and group management in technology mediated services. *Personnel Psychology, 63*(2), 265-298.

Malone, C. (2024). *Artificial intelligence in the hotel industry: The benefits and effects.* Human Nutrition and Hospitality Management Undergraduate Honors Theses, University of Arkansas.

Maslach, C., Schaufeli, W. B., & Leiter, M. P. (2001). Job burnout. *Annual Review of Psychology, 52*(1), 397-422.

McLean, G. N., Yang, B., Kuo, M. H. C., Tolbert, A. S., & Larkin, C. (2005). Development and initial validation of an instrument measuring managerial coaching skill. *Human Resource Development Quarterly, 16*(2), 157-178.

Mesmer-Magnus, J. R., & Viswesvaran, C. (2005). Convergence between measures of work-to-family and family-to-work conflict. *Journal of Vocational Behavior, 67*(2), 215-232.

Nembhard, I. M., & Edmondson, A. C. (2006). Making it safe: The effects of leader inclusiveness and professional status on psychological safety and improvement efforts. *Journal of Organizational Behavior, 27*(7), 941-966.

NetSuite. (2025). *AI in hospitality: Advantages and use cases.* Retrieved from https://www.netsuite.com

O'Neill, J. W., & Xiao, Q. (2010). The role of brand affiliation in hotel market value. *Cornell Hospitality Quarterly, 51*(3), 427-446.

OysterLink. (2025). *Hospitality industry worker burnout report 2025.* OysterLink Research.

Paychex. (2023). *Employee burnout by industry survey.* Paychex Research Institute.

People Management Association. (2022). *Cost of employee turnover study.* HR Research Institute.

Planday. (2024). *The burnout crisis in hospitality.* Retrieved from https://www.planday.com

Schein, E. H. (1978). *Career dynamics: Matching individual and organizational needs.* Boston: Addison Wesley.

Schein, E. H. (1985). *Organizational culture and leadership.* San Francisco: Jossey Bass.

Schön, D. A. (1983). *The reflective practitioner: How professionals think in action.* New York: Basic Books.

Sheridan, J. E. (1992). Organizational culture and employee retention. *Academy of Management Journal, 35*(5), 1036-1056.

Singh, A., & Sharma, R. (2024). Embracing the new era: Artificial intelligence and its multifaceted impact on the hospitality industry. *Technology in Society, 79,* 102357.

Super, D. E. (1980). A life span, life space approach to career development. *Journal of Vocational Behavior, 16*(3), 282-298.

Thompson, T., Foreman, P., & Martin, F. (1998). Impostor fears and perfectionistic concern over mistakes. *Personality and Individual Differences, 28*(4), 629-637.

U.S. Bureau of Labor Statistics. (2023). *Job openings and labor turnover survey.* U.S. Department of Labor.

Vergauwe, J., Wille, B., Feys, M., De Fruyt, F., & Anseel, F. (2015). Fear of being exposed: The trait-relatedness of the impostor phenomenon and its relevance in the work context. *Journal of Business and Psychology, 30*(3), 565-581.

Vygotsky, L. S. (1978). *Mind in society: The development of higher psychological processes.* Cambridge, MA: Harvard University Press.

Whitmore, J. (2009). *Coaching for performance* (4th ed.). London: Nicholas Brealey.

Wong, C. A., & Laschinger, H. K. (2013). Authentic leadership, performance, and job satisfaction. *Journal of Advanced Nursing, 69*(4), 947-959.

Work Institute. (2023). *2023 Retention report.* Franklin, TN: Work Institute.

Workhuman. (2023). *The impact of wellness programs on employee burnout.* Workhuman Research Institute.

Zenger, J. H., & Stinnett, K. (2010). *The extraordinary coach: How the best leaders help others grow.* New York: McGraw-Hill.

Professional Biography

With over 35 years in the hospitality industry, Mr. Nelson serves as Human Resource Director in Portland, Oregon, where he combines decades of hands-on experience with rigorous academic research. His career has taken him across the globe, from living in the Middle East to traveling extensively through Europe, cultivating a deep curiosity about how people experience the world around them. These international perspectives have shaped his approach to leadership and human connection.

Mr. Nelson holds a Master of Business Administration in Human Resources from Louisiana State University in Shreveport, Louisiana, and is currently pursuing a Doctorate in Industrial and Organizational Psychology with a qualitative focus. His research centers on developing best practices for hotel and resort organizational structures, with his dissertation examining how leadership behaviors in the hospitality industry influence employee turnover intentions. This work bridges his professional expertise with academic inquiry, seeking answers to the challenges he has witnessed firsthand throughout his career.

Beyond the boardroom and classroom, Mr. Nelson has been married to his best friend for over 30 years and is a proud father of four and grandfather of four. Family remains his anchor, informing his belief that successful organizations are built on the same principles that sustain strong families: trust, communication, and mutual growth.

Looking ahead, Mr. Nelson envisions creating a comprehensive training platform designed to develop the next generation of hospitality leaders. He plans to publish leadership books that translate research into practical wisdom and continue delivering lectures at universities nationwide. His mission is clear: equip aspiring leaders with the skills, insights, and character necessary to transform the hospitality industry from within.